Mike McGrath

LINUX

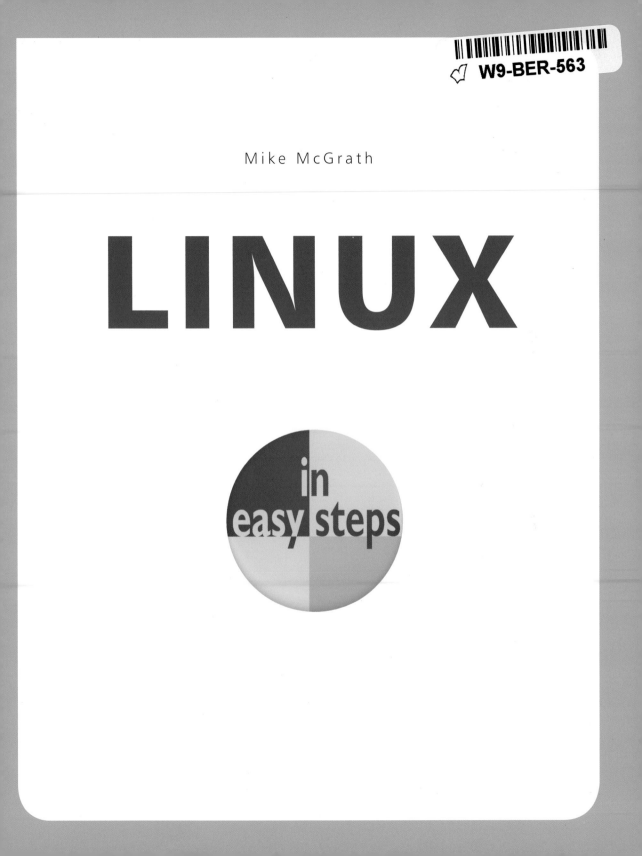

in
easy steps

In easy steps is an imprint of Computer Step
Southfield Road · Southam
Warwickshire CV47 0FB · United Kingdom
www.ineasysteps.com

Fourth Edition

Notice of Liability
Every effort has been made to ensure that this book contains accurate
and current information. However, Computer Step and the author
shall not be liable for any loss or damage suffered by readers as a
result of any information contained herein.

Trademarks
All trademarks are acknowledged as belonging to their respective
companies.

Printed and bound in the United Kingdom

ISBN-13 978-1-84078-351-3
ISBN-10 1-84078-351-6

Contents

Guess what? Wheels have been round for a really long time, and anybody who "reinvents" the new wheel is generally considered a crackpot. It turns out that "round" is simply a good form for a wheel to have. It may be boring, but it just tends to roll better than a square, and "hipness" has nothing what-so-ever to do with it.

Linus Torvalds, creator of the Linux kernel

1 Getting started

This chapter introduces the Linux operating system and describes a typical installation process.

Introducing Linux

Linux is a computer operating system that can run on a variety of hardware including the popular Intel system found on most desktop computers. It is a modern derivation of the powerful Unix operating system that was introduced way back in 1969.
In recent years the popularity of Linux has increased dramatically as computer users have discovered its many benefits:

Hot tip

Pronounce the name Linux with a short "i" – so it's "li-nucks" not "lie-nucks".

- Linux is released under the GNU General Public License that ensures it remains free to all users – no-one can charge for this operating system so you will never have to pay for it. It's available for free download on the Internet but you may have to pay a distribution charge if you prefer a copy on CD/DVD

- Access to the source code of Linux is unrestricted and it may be changed. This has allowed thousands of programmers around the world to refine the code to improve performance

- Linux is truly a multi-user, multi-tasking operating system that allows multiple users to simultaneously work with multiple applications without experiencing any traffic problems. Many of the world's web servers run on Linux for this very reason

- Linux is an extremely stable operating system – continuous uptimes of more than a year are not uncommon. It can be upgraded "on the fly" so it only needs a reboot to add hardware

Don't forget

Many web servers are said to have a "LAMP" configuration – an acronym for Linux, Apache, MySQL, PHP.

- There are a large number of quality applications available to run on the Linux platform. These are comparable to commercial applications that run on other operating systems but, like Linux, these too are free of charge. For instance, the free OpenOffice suite offers similar functionality to the Microsoft Office suite

- With open-source software an administrator can know exactly what a program can do and the security dangers it presents. An open-source application cannot secretly gather information about the user or send confidential information to third parties

The evolution of Linux

In 1983 a visionary programmer named Richard Stallman began a movement called the GNU Project. Its philosophy was that software should be free from restrictions against copying or modification in order to make better and efficient programs. This inspired programmers around the world to create programs driven by efficiency rather than by financial incentive.

Hot tip

The term "GNU" is a recursive acronym for GNU's Not Unix.

By 1991 the GNU Project had created a lot of software tools including the GNU C Compiler written by Stallman himself. At that time many of these tools were incorporated into a Unix-compatible operating system by a 21-year old student at the University of Helsinki. His name was Linus Torvalds and he named the operating system Linux (LINUs - uniX).

Linux was made available for download on the Internet so other programmers could test and tweak the source code, then return it to Linus Torvalds. After a period of enthusiastic development Linux 1.0 was made available globally under the GNU General Public License which ensured it would remain free.

Programmers were keen to explore Linux and soon found some amazing uses for it. In April 1996, researchers at Los Alamos National Laboratory used Linux to run 68 PCs as a single parallel processing machine to simulate atomic shock waves. At $150,000 this supercomputer cost just 1-tenth the price of a comparable commercial machine. It reached a peak speed of 19 billion calculations per second, making it the 315th most powerful supercomputer in the world. It proved to be robust too – three months later it still didn't have to be rebooted.

Linux continued to grow in popularity as a text-based operating system while Windows became the dominant graphical desktop operating system. Recognizing that most PC users want the point-and-click convenience of a graphical environment, the Linux camp began to develop a system comparable to the Windows desktop.

From a handful of enthusiasts in 1991 to millions of users now – Linux has come of age. Today's sleek K Desktop Environment (KDE) and the Gnome environment now offer a user-friendly alternative for Windows users – Linux for the desktop!

Choosing a Linux distro

At the very heart of Linux is a bunch of tried and tested compiled code called the "kernel". The kernel provides the operating system with its core functionality, much like the engine in a car. It takes care of the basics, such as helping other programs access hardware and sharing your computer's processor among various programs.

In addition to the kernel, Linux contains a number of system-level programs, such as the services to handle your email, web connection and bootloader. Consider these as a car's transmission, gears, and chassis – without these the engine is not much use.

Linux distributions generally also include a large number of user-level programs – the applications for daily use. For instance, web browsers, word processors, text editors, graphics editors, media players, and so on. These are the finishing touches to the car that ensure a great ride – whitewall tires and soft leather upholstery.

All of these components are bundled together in a wide variety of Linux distribution packages, commonly referred to as "distros". Just as all the components of a car are bundled together to make a complete car.

In the same way that there are many makes and models of cars there are many Linux distros to choose from. The most well known distros are RedHat, SuSE, PCLinuxOS and Ubuntu. Each distro has its own installer and unique default configuration according to what the distributor considers to be the best arrangement. The ideal one for you will depend on your own personal preferences and how you want to use Linux. The most popular distros are described below to help you choose.

Hot tip

The openSUSE, PCLinuxOS, and Ubuntu distros are each available as a "live" version that lets you run Linux from a disk – so you can try it out without installing Linux on your hard drive.

10

RedHat Fedora

One of the most publicized Linux distros comprising the commercial RedHat Enterprise Linux product line and the unsupported free Fedora Core distro that is developed by the community, serving as a test base for RedHat Enterprise Linux.
Pros: Widely used, excellent community support, innovative.
Cons: Limited product life-span of the free edition, poor multimedia support.
Free download at **http://www.fedoraproject.org**.

Novell SUSE

The community-based openSUSE distro, sponsored by Novell, is another distro with desktop focus which has received positive reviews for its installer and YaST configuration tools. The documentation, which comes with the boxed product, has been labeled as the most complete, thorough and usable by far. This distro provides the base for Novell's award-winning SUSE Linux Enterprise products

Pros: Attention to detail, easy-to-use YaST configuration tools
Cons: Huge distro – including over 1,500 bundled packages
Free download at **http://www.opensuse.org**.

PCLinuxOS

A polished community edition based on the Mandriva Linux distro, which uses the K Desktop Environment (KDE) to manage the graphical user interface (GUI). The slogan "radically simple" describes its intention to be the most user-friendly distro for users migrating from the Windows operating system. The PCLinuxOS distro is gaining much popularity due to its instant familiarity and support for many media formats straight out of the box – including MP3, Quicktime and Microsoft's **wmv** format.

Pros: User-friendly interface, good native multimedia support.
Cons: Smaller community than more established distros.
Free download at **http://www.pclinuxos.com**.

Ubuntu

This sophisticated community distro employs the popular Gnome GUI desktop manager. It has the advantage of a fixed six-month release cycle and a clearly set product lifetime of 18 months. Ubuntu provides great documentation and offers free CDs with free shipping to anywhere in the world. It does not include proprietary media codecs, to comply with legal requirements, but provides a one-click facility to add them on demand after installation. At the time of writing this edition is acknowledged to be the most popular Linux distro – so is used throughout this book to describe the many features of the Linux operating system.

Pros: Great community of developers and users, fixed release cycle
Cons: Default color scheme is brown – but this is easily changed.
Free download at **http://ubuntulinux.org**.

Evaluating hardware

Before installing Linux on a computer it is necessary to evaluate its hardware specifications for suitability. The table below suggests minimum specifications for processor, memory and hard disk (HD) drive.

Hardware item	Suggested minimum
CPU speed	300Mhz – 1.0Ghz+ is better
RAM memory size	128Mb – 256Mb+ is better
HD drive capacity	5Gb – 10Gb+ is better

It's easy to discover the CPU, RAM memory information, and HD capacity if Windows is already installed on the computer:

 Click on the Start button, then the Control Panel menu item to launch the Control Panel folder window

 In the Control Panel, click the System icon to launch the System window on Windows Vista (the System dialog on Windows XP)

Read the Processor and RAM values, comparing them to the minimum requirements in the table above

Don't forget

If you're using Windows XP the settings are on the General tab in the System dialog.

4 Click on the Start button, then the Computer menu item (My Computer on Windows XP) to launch the Computer folder window

5 In the Computer window select the View, Details menus

6 Compare the Total Size and Free Space values to the minimum requirements in the table opposite.

Consideration should also be given to the hardware used to connect to the Internet. Connection via a PCI ethernet card, or on-motherboard ethernet controller, is very well supported in Linux and virtually all hardware of this type is suitable.

Unfortunately modems are rather more problematic. Many computers are supplied with an internal PCI modem that will only work with Windows software. These so-called "winmodems" are unsuitable for connection to the Internet in Linux. If you have an internal modem and find it is unusable in Linux you will probably have to replace it with different hardware before you can connect to the Internet. Usually the easiest solution is to connect an external modem via a traditional RS232 serial port.

Hot tip

If you are really determined to try to get a winmodem working in Linux visit **www.linmodems.org** for lots of useful advice.

13

Making space for Linux

An operating system is installed on an area of the HD drive called a "partition". When Windows is the only installed operating system its partition will normally occupy the entire HD drive. To install Linux in this situation there are three possible options:

1 **Delete the Windows partition** – replacing it with Linux partitions that occupy the entire drive. This option will delete the Windows operating system along with all the applications and data files. It creates a dedicated Linux computer which will immediately start Linux when the PC gets switched on.

2 **Reduce the Windows partition size** – so that it no longer occupies the entire drive, then create Linux partitions in the resulting free space. This option will retain the Windows operating system, applications and data files. It creates a "dual-boot" computer that allows the user to choose whether to start Linux or Windows whenever the PC gets switched on.

3 **Add a second HD drive to the system** – this allows Linux partitions to occupy the entire second drive and retains the Windows operating system, applications and data files on the first drive. It too creates a dual-boot computer that allows the user to choose whether to start Linux or Windows whenever the PC gets switched on.

Beware

Resizing partitions is a scary process where data loss can, and does, occur – even in expert hands. All contents of the partition must be backed up before attempting this operation.

The option to install an additional HD drive for Linux is a popular choice for many people as they have often upgraded their original HD drive to a larger one, and so have their original drive spare. It also has several benefits over the other options:

● The free space on the Windows drive is not reduced

● It removes the risk of data loss through partition resizing

● The familiar Windows operating system is retained

● It distinctly separates the two operating systems

● Drive failure would only disrupt one operating system

Adding a second HD drive

Most modern PCs can accommodate up to four EIDE (Enhanced Integrated Device Electronics) devices, such as HD drives and CD /DVD drives, but typically ship with just two – one HD drive and one CD drive. This means that one or two more drives can be added simply by plugging them into the existing system.

The first HD drive in a system is known as the "Master" HD drive and a second HD drive is called the "Slave" HD drive.

A "jumper" connects two tiny pins to determine if the drive should be regarded as a Master (MA) drive or Slave (SL) drive. The top of each HD drive usually has a diagram depicting which pins need to be connected in each case.

Hot tip

If you are not comfortable working inside your PC case a computer store should be pleased to undertake the fitting of a second drive for a modest fee.

1 Ensure that the jumper on the original drive is set to Master, then set the jumper on the second drive to Slave

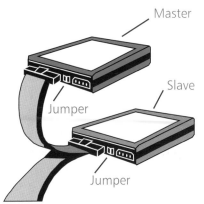

Master

Slave

Jumper

Jumper

2 Connect the wide data cable to the Master HD drive, by the plug at the end of the cable – not the plug part way along the cable

3 Now connect the data cable to the Slave HD drive, by the plug part way along the cable

4 Connect the power cables to both drives, then close the PC case

5 Start up the PC and check that both drives are now detected by the system – if the second drive is not detected change the BIOS settings to "auto-seek" it when booting up.

Beginning installation

If you choose to install Linux on the same HD drive as Windows, it's a good idea to clean up the disk before starting the installation.

 Click on the Start button, then the Computer menu item (My Computer on Windows XP) to launch the Computer folder window

2 Right-click on the HD drive icon and select Properties from the context menu to launch the Properties dialog

3 Choose the Tools tab in the Properties dialog then click the Check Now button to open the Check Disk dialog

4 In the Check Disk dialog, select both options then click its Start button to schedule a disk check – you may now need to restart your computer to run the scheduled check

Check Disk (C:)

Check disk options
☑ Automatically fix file system errors
☑ Scan for and attempt recovery of bad sectors

Start   Cancel

 When the disk check has completed, click on the Defragment Now button in the Properties dialog to tidy up the file system – after the defragmenter has rearranged the files on the hard disk you're ready to install Linux

(C:) Properties

General | Tools | Hardware | Sharing | Security | Quota

Error-checking
This option will check the volume for errors.

Check Now...

Defragmentation
This option will defragment files on the volume.

Defragment Now...

6 Download your favorite Linux distro then burn it as a filesystem image on an empty CD disk. For example download Ubuntu from **www.ubuntu.com/download** – or order it on a free CD from **www.ubuntu.com**

Linux installations begin by booting the computer from the CD. This requires the computer BIOS (Basic Input/Output System) settings to seek boot instructions from the CD drive before using those on the HD drive. If your computer looks to boot from the HD drive first you will need to change the BIOS settings.

7 Open the BIOS Setup Utility (typically by holding down the Delete key right after the memory test when the computer is first switched on) then locate the boot device order in the advanced BIOS features

8 Make the CD drive the First Boot Device, and the HD drive the Second Boot Device – then save the settings and exit the BIOS Setup Utility

9 Place the Linux image disk in the CD drive then start the computer to see a boot prompt screen load from the CD disk

10 Select the menu option to "Check CD for Defects" to run a check on the integrity of your CD disk – this should be performed to be sure there are no errors on the disk

11 When the disk check completes without errors, choose the menu option "Start or Install Ubuntu" – Linux then loads entirely in RAM memory and displays a working desktop without changing anything on the HD drive

12 Click the "Install" icon that is displayed on the desktop to begin the procedure to install Linux on the HD drive

Hot tip

Help on burning a filesystem image can be found at **https://wiki.ubuntu.com/ BurningIsoHowto**.

Hot tip

Like Ubuntu, many Linux distros have a "Live CD" that let you initially try out Linux without installing anything on your HD drive.

Partitioning the disk

The Linux installer begins by asking you to select the language you prefer to use during the installation process, your location, and keyboard layout, before moving on to partitioning the HD drive. This prepares the disk by creating a partition for the Linux operating system and a swap partition for dynamic processes.

Beware

The default partitioning option will overwrite anything that is currently on the HD drive.

1 If you wish to use the entire HD drive for Linux, accept the default option – set to create a small swap partition and a further partition occupying the rest of the disk

Install

Prepare disk space

How do you want to partition the disk?

⦿ Guided - use entire disk

⦿ IDE1 master (hda) - 41.1 GB Maxtor 2F040J0

○ Manual

Cancel   Back   Forward

2 Alternatively, select the "Manual" option – then click the Forward button to launch the custom partitioning dialog

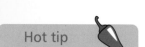

Hot tip

Separating the operating system and user files allows Linux to be reinstalled while retaining the user's data.

Install

Prepare partitions

Device	Type	Mount point	Format?	Size	Used
/dev/hda					
free space			☐	41110 MB	

New partition   Undo changes to partitions

3 Select the "free space" item – then click the New Partition button to launch the Create Partition dialog

4 Specify a Primary Swap partition, of a size roughly double that of the RAM memory installed on your system, then click OK to update the Prepare Partition settings

---

Create partition

Create a new partition

Type for the new partition:	● Primary ○ Logical
New partition size in megabytes (1000000 bytes):	1024
Location for the new partition:	● Beginning ○ End
Use as:	swap
Mount point:	

❌ Cancel   ⏎ OK

4 Select the free space now remaining, then click the New Partition button again and specify a 10Gb partition of type "ext3" with a mount point of "/" – this will contain the Linux operating system and allow space for additions

5 Select the free space now remaining, then click the New Partition button once more and specify another partition to occupy all remaining disk space. This should also be of type "ext3" but with a mount point of "/home" – to contain all the user-created files. The partition table settings should now look something like those below:

Install

Prepare partitions

Device	Type	Mount point	Format?	Size	Used
/dev/hda					
/dev/hda1	swap		☐	1024 MB	unknown
/dev/hda2	ext3	/	☑	10002 MB	unknown
/dev/hda3	ext3	/home	☑	30084 MB	unknown

New partition table   Undo changes to partitions

19

Creating a user account

When you are satisfied with the partition table settings the installer next looks for a Windows partition and offers to import documents and those from Windows to your Linux system. Where this is appropriate you must create a Linux user account, by entering a user name, login name, and password, into which the documents and settings will be imported. Where no Windows partition is present there will, of course, be nothing to import:

1   Enter the user details for import if appropriate then click the Forward button to launch the default user account setup dialog

2   Type your actual name into the top text box – for example "Mike McGrath"

3   In the next text box type a short lowercase login name for the user – such as "mike"

4   Now type a password that will be required each time this user wants to login to the Linux system

5 Choose a name to uniquley identify this particular computer when connected to a network and type it in the final text box – for example "mikes-desktop"

Install _ □ ✕

Who are you?

What is your name?

> Mike McGrath

What name do you want to use to log in?

> mike

If more than one person will use this computer, you can set up multiple accounts after installation.

Choose a password to keep your account safe.

> ✱✱✱✱✱✱   ✱✱✱✱✱✱

Enter the same password twice, so that it can be checked for typing errors.

What is the name of this computer?

> mikes-desktop

This name will be used if you make the computer visible to others on a network.

Step 6 of 7   ✖ Cancel   ⬅ Back   ➡ Forward

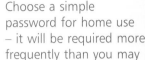

Hot tip

Choose a simple password for home use – it will be required more frequently than you may now think.

Up to this point in the installation process no changes have actually been made to the system – you have merely been entering configuration settings that will be used to partition the HD drive and install Linux with a default user account.

6 Now make sure that all peripheral devices that will be used by Linux are connected to the computer and are switched on. For example, printer, scanner, and internet connection. This will ensure they can be recognized and the system configured for them during installation

7 Press the Forward button to proceed

Don't forget

More users can be added later and passwords can be changed later.

Completing installation

Just before installation begins the installer displays a summary of the configuration settings, allowing a final check prior to installation. If any changes are needed the Back button can be used to return to the appropriate dialog where the configuration can be amended.

Install ⎯ ☐ ✕

Ready to install

Your new operating system will now be installed with the following settings:

Language: English
Keyboard layout: U.S. English
Name: Mike McGrath
Login name: mike
Location: America/New_York
Migration Assistant:

If you continue, the changes listed below will be written to the disks. Otherwise, you will be able to make further changes manually.

WARNING: This will destroy all data on any partitions you have removed as well as on the partitions that are going to be formatted.

The partition tables of the following devices are changed:
IDE1 master (hda)

The following partitions are going to be formatted:
partition #1 of IDE1 master (hda) as swap
partition #2 of IDE1 master (hda) as ext3
partition #3 of IDE1 master (hda) as ext3

Advanced...

Step 7 of 7   ✗ Cancel   ⬅ Back   ➡ Install

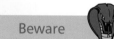

Beware

Check the summary very carefully before proceeding – the next step will format your hard drive and apply your selections.

 When you are completely satisfied with the summary, click on the Install button to partition the HD drive and to install the Linux system

Installing system

Partitions formatting

5%

Creating ext3 file system for / in partition #2 of IDE1 master (hda)...

Installing system

Installing system

45%

Copying files...

2　After the installation completes a dialog box appears advising you that the computer must now be restarted – click on the "Restart now" button

Installation complete

Installation is complete. You need to restart the computer in order to use the new installation. You can continue to use this live CD, although any changes you make or documents you save will not be preserved.

Be sure to remove the CD when restarting the computer, otherwise it will start back up using this live CD rather than the newly-installed system.

Continue using the live CD　　Restart now

3　Soon a message prompts you to remove the CD so the system will restart from the files installed on the HD drive – remove the CD then hit the Return key

4　When the system reboots it will request you to login – enter the user name and password created during the installation process to load your new Linux desktop

Don't forget

The installation speed will depend on your system – this system took around twenty minutes.

Summary

- Linux is a free stable multi-user operating system that is derived from the powerful Unix operating system

- The name "Linux" combines letters from the first name of its originator, Linus Torvalds, with the "x" in Unix

- Both KDE and the Gnome desktop are user-friendly graphical user interfaces, providing the same point-and-click convenience of the Windows desktop

- The kernel provides the core functionality of Linux

- Distros bundle the kernel, system-level programs, and free user-level programs in a variety of combinations

- The Ubuntu distro employs the Gnome desktop manager and enjoys widespread popularity

- Minimum hardware requirements to run Linux are a CPU speed of 300Mhz, RAM of 128Mb, and a 5Gb HD drive – but higher specifications will perform better

- A second HD drive can easily be added to a PC so it can dual-boot to Linux or Windows

- Before installing Linux alongside Windows it is recommended that the HD drive be checked for errors and defragmented

- A Linux distro can often be downloaded from the internet and burned as a filesystem image onto a single installation CD

- In order to boot from a CD it may be necessary to change the boot device order using the BIOS Setup Utility

- The Linux installer will, by default, create a small swap partition and a second partition occupying all other disk space

- Creating a custom partition for user data allows Linux to be reinstalled later without affecting users' saved files

- The name and password of the user account created during installation are required to login to the Linux desktop

2 Exploring the desktop

This chapter demonstrates how to customize a Linux desktop to your preference.

Adjusting the taskbar

After booting Linux, and entering the user name and password created during installation, the new Linux desktop will appear.

The default Ubuntu desktop has a taskbar panel across the top of the screen and a secondary panel across the bottom of the screen. The items on these panels can be united into a single taskbar in the more conventional location at the bottom of the screen.

1 Click on the taskbar and hold down the mouse button while dragging the taskbar to the bottom of the screen

2 Right-click on the taskbar, then choose "Add to Panel" from the context menu – to launch the Add to Panel dialog that is used to add items to desktop panels

3 Click on the "Show Desktop" icon then the "Add" button to add a Show Desktop button to the taskbar – duplicating the button at the left of the secondary panel

Hot tip

Right-click on the taskbar and choose Properties, then check the Autohide option on the General Tab of the Properties dialog to hide the taskbar when not in use.

Add to Panel

Select an item to add to the panel
(you can also directly drag and drop items onto the panel):

Search: [   ]

☐ Application Launcher... ☐ Custom Application Launcher

Desktop & Windows

Drawer Force Quit Lock Screen Quit... Show Desktop

Trash Window List Window Selector Switcher Workspace Switcher

Hide application windows and show the desktop

❷ Help   ◀ Back   ✚ Add   ✖ Close

Beware

The Window List item
is not apparent until a
window is open – but
without it a minimalized
window can seem to
completely disappear!

4 Now add a Window List, Workspace Switcher, and Trash
button to the taskbar – duplicating the remaining items
on the secondary panel

5 Right-click on the secondary panel, then choose "Delete
this Panel" from the context menu to remove the panel

6 Right click on the Show
Desktop button that
has been added to the
taskbar then choose
"Move" from the context
menu and move it to
your preferred position

❷ Help

🗔 Get Help Online...
🗎 Translate This Application...
🔧 Report a Problem

ℹ About

— Remove From Panel
  Move
  Lock To Panel

Don't forget

You can add extra panels
at any time – right-click
on the taskbar and
choose New Panel from
the context menu.

7 Repeat the previous step for each of the taskbar items
until you are satisfied with the taskbar layout

Applications Places System   Mike McGrath   Wed Oct 31, 6:26 AM

Window List   Workspace Switcher   Trash   Show Desktop

27

Launching applications

Applications are launched from the Linux desktop using a "Applications" menu and additional launchers can easily be added to the taskbar and desktop for frequently used applications.

 Click the Applications button, at the far left of the taskbar, then position the mouse pointer over the Accessories item to open that menu

 On the Accessories menu, click the Text Editor item to launch the Text Editor

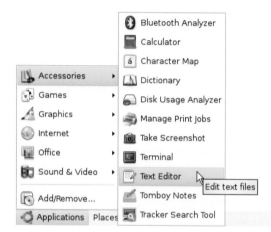

Don't forget

The menus shown here are from the Ubuntu distro – those on other distros will vary.

Right-click on the Text Editor item in the Accessories menu then choose "Add this launcher to panel" from the context menu to create a launcher button on the taskbar

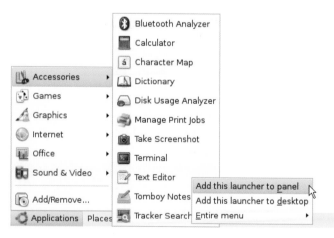

4 Click the new launcher that has been added to the taskbar to launch the Text Editor

5 Right-click on the Text Editor item in the Accessories menu then choose "Add this launcher to desktop" from the context menu to create a launcher icon on the desktop

6 Click the shortcut launcher icon that has been added to the desktop to launch the Text Editor

You can also create a desktop launcher icon for any application if you know its precise name. In this instance the Text Editor for the Gnome desktop is named "gedit".

7 Right-click anywhere on the desktop, then choose "Create Launcher" from the context menu that appears

8 Type a name and the **gedit** Command into the appropriate input fields in the Create Launcher dialog, then click its OK button to create the desktop launcher

Hot tip

Applications can also be launched from the command line – see page 108 for details.

Changing screen resolution

Many features of your Linux system can be customized to your preference using the System, Preferences menu from the taskbar. The installation process should have selected a screen resolution that is appropriate for your monitor but you can easily change this if you prefer an alternative resolution.

1 Click the System button on the taskbar, then position the pointer over the Preferences item to launch that menu

2 On the Preferences menu, click the Screen Resolution item to launch the Screen Resolution Preferences dialog

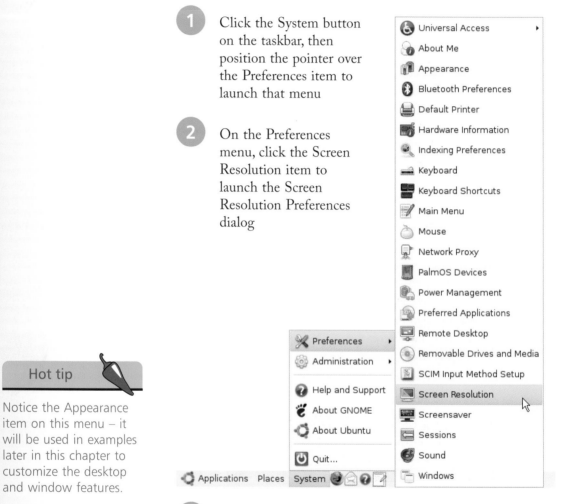

Hot tip

Notice the Appearance item on this menu – it will be used in examples later in this chapter to customize the desktop and window features.

3 In the Screen Resolution Preferences dialog, click the arrowed button to the right of the current Resolution setting to display a list of alternative resolutions

Screen Resolution Preferences

Default Settings

Resolution: 1024x768

Refresh rate: 60 Hz

Rotation: Normal

Options

☐ Make default for this computer only

? Help   ✕ Close   ✓ Apply

4 Select your preferred resolution from the list of alternatives, then click the Apply button to change the screen to the new resolution

Screen Resolution Preferences

Default Settings

Resolution: 1280x800

1280x768

Refresh rate: 1024x768

800x600

Rotation: 640x480

Options

☐ Make default for this computer only

? Help   ✕ Close   ✓ Apply

31

5 After changing the screen resolution a dialog box appears containing a countdown message. If you are happy with the new appearance click the Keep Resolution button to prevent your system reverting to the previous resolution when the countdown ends

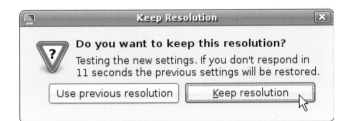

Keep Resolution

Do you want to keep this resolution?

? Testing the new settings. If you don't respond in 11 seconds the previous settings will be restored.

Use previous resolution   Keep resolution

Choosing a background

One of the first changes many people want to make to their new Linux desktop is to install a custom desktop background from the selection of free "wallpaper" images available on the internet.

1 Click Applications, Internet, Firefox Web Browser, then type "desktop wallpaper" into the browser's Search field and hit Return

G ▾ desktop wallpaper

2 From the search results, find a wallpaper image to suit your screen resolution then right-click on the image and choose "Save Image As..." from the brower context menu

Copy Image Location
Save Image As...
Send Image...
Properties
Switch Page Direction

3 Use the arrowed button in the "Save in folder" field to set the location to the Pictures folder, then click Save

Save Image

Name: africa.jpeg

Save in folder: 📁 Pictures

▷ Browse for other folders

✗ Cancel   💾 Save

4 Right-click anywhere on the desktop, then choose "Change Desktop Background" from the context menu to launch the Appearance Preferences dialog box

📁 Create Folder
   Create Launcher...
📄 Create Document   ▸

   Clean Up by Name
✓ Keep Aligned

📋 Paste

   Change Desktop Background

32

Appearance Preferences

Theme | **Background** | Fonts | Interface | Desktop Effects

Wallpaper

Style: Fill screen

+ Add...   − Remove

Colors

Solid color

? Help   ✕ Close

Hot tip

Notice that the thumbnail version of the current desktop background is outlined.

The Appearance Preferences dialog contains thumbnail versions of possible desktop wallpaper images.

5 In the Appearance Preferences dialog, click the Add button to launch the Add Wallpaper dialog

6 In the Add Wallpaper dialog choose the Pictures folder in the places field then select your wallpaper and click Open – your desktop background changes instantly to your chosen wallpaper image and a thumbnail version gets added to the Appearance Preferences dialog

Add Wallpaper

📄 | ◀ | mike | **Pictures**

Places
- Documents
- Music
- Pictures
- Videos

Name
- africa.jpeg

+ Add   − Remove

Images

✕ Cancel   Open

Beware

The left-most wallpaper in the Appearance Preferences dialog is not an image. It represents a solid color selection and can be modified by the dialog's Colors button. Do not remove this solid color wallpaper.

Customizing windows

The Appearance Preferences dialog, that was introduced in the previous example, allows you to choose exactly how you want your windows to look.

1 Open the Appearance Preferences dialog as before or with System, Preferences, Appearance from the taskbar, then click on its Theme tab

Hot tip

More themes can be downloaded from the internet and added to the theme selection using the Install button. Try www.gnome-look.org for more themes.

2 Click on any pre-installed theme thumbnail to instantly change all controls, colors, window borders, icons, and pointers, to those specified by that theme

3 Click on the "Human" theme to return to the default Ubuntu theme once more

4 Now click on the Customize button to begin creating your own theme in the Customize Theme dialog

5 In the Customize Theme dialog, click on the "Industrial" option in the Controls tab – the window appearance immediately changes to the new settings

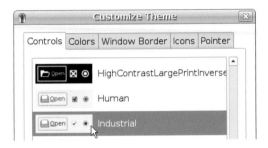

6 Click the Colors tab then the Selected Items Background button to launch the Pick a Color dialog – choose a red

7 Click the OK button to apply the color to the windows and to close the Pick a Color dialog

8 In the Customize Theme dialog, click the Close button to close that dialog box

9 In the Appearance Preferences dialog click the Save As button then name your new theme "Red Industrial" in the Save Theme As dialog – a thumbnail of this theme gets added to the Theme tab for selection at any time

Don't forget

You can further customize your themes by selecting options on the other tabs.

35

Enabling system sounds

If you prefer to hear audible acknowledgements as you work on
your Linux desktop, system sounds can be enabled using the
Sound Preferences dialog.

 On the taskbar, click System, Preferences, then the Sound
item – to launch the Sound Preferences dialog

In the Sound Preferences dialog, click the Sounds tab
then ensure that both options are checked to "Enable
software sound mixing" and "Play system sounds"

Sound Preferences

Devices | Sounds | System Beep

☑ Enable software sound mixing (ESD)
☑ Play system sounds

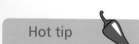

Hot tip

You can test the sound
devices on your system
using the Test buttons
on the Devices tab of the
Sound Preference dialog.

On the Sounds tab, click the arrowed button against one
of the System events to display a list of possible sounds

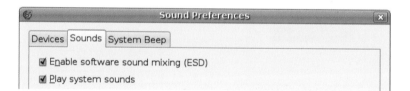

System Sounds

Select check box:	No sound	▷ Play
Choose menu item:	No sound	▷ Play
Click on command button:	No sound	▷ Play
Miscellaneous message:	No sound	▷ Play
Question dialog:	No sound	▷ Play
Error message:	No sound	▷ Play

4 From the list of sounds
that appears, select an
appropriate sound for
that event – the list
disappears, the sound
name is added and the
Play button gets enabled

| Login |
| Logout |
| **Boing** |
| Siren |
| Clink |
| Beep |
| No sound |
| Select sound file... |

5 Click the Play button to hear the selected sound

System Sounds

Select check box: Boing   ⇕   ▷ Play

Choose menu item: No sound   ⇕   ▷ Play

6 Click the arrowed
button against another
System event, but this
time select the option to
"Select sound file..." to
launch the Select Sound
File dialog – choose
any sound file on your
system

| Login |
| Logout |
| Boing |
| Siren |
| Clink |
| Beep |
| No sound |
| **Select sound file...** |

7 Click the Play button to hear the chosen sound file

System Sounds

Select check box: Boing   ⇕   ▷ Play

Choose menu item: clicked.wav   ⇕   ▷ Play

Don't forget

After choosing a sound
for each system event
listed you can turn all
sounds off at any time
by unchecking the option
to "Play system sounds"
– and turn them back on
later by re-checking it.

8 If necessary the volume can
be adjusted using the volume
control on the taskbar – just
click the volume button then
drag the slider

◀ Fri Aug 24, 1:10 PM ⏻

Using multiple desktops

One great feature of Linux desktops not found in Windows is the ability to support multiple "virtual" desktops. This allows you to open applications on different desktops and to easily switch between those running applications.

The Ubunti installer provides two virtual desktops, which are depicted on the taskbar as a simple block of two square buttons. This block is the "workspace switcher" that represents the default desktop on the left button and a second desktop on the right button – clicking these buttons will switch between desktops.

Workspace switcher buttons display an icon of the application running on that desktop when the window size is full screen. Otherwise the size and position of each window is depicted. Additional workspaces can be added, up to a total of 36, but four virtual desktops is usually sufficient for most situations.

1. Right-click on the workspace switcher and choose the Preferences item from the context menu – to launch the Workspace Switcher Preferences dialog

📄 <u>P</u>references
❓ <u>H</u>elp
⊗ Get Help Online...
📋 Translate This Application...
✻ Report a Problem
ℹ <u>A</u>bout
⊟ <u>R</u>emove From Panel
Move
Loc<u>k</u> To Panel

Hot tip

If you prefer to have names on the switcher buttons edit the workspace names and check the option to "Show workspace names in switcher" at the bottom of the preferences dialog.

2. In the Workspace Switcher Preferences dialog, use the arrowed button in the workspaces field to increase the number of workspaces to four

Workspace Switcher Preferences

Switcher
- ○ Show <u>o</u>nly the current workspace
- ● Show <u>a</u>ll workspaces in: `1` ⬍ rows

Workspaces
Number of <u>w</u>orkspaces: `4` ⬍

Workspace na<u>m</u>es:

Desk 1
Desk 2

3 Click the Close button to close the Workspace Switcher Preferences dialog – the workspace switcher on the taskbar now has four buttons

4 Launch the Firefox web browser from the Applications, Internet menu, ensuring its window is maximised on desktop one, then click the next button along the switcher

Don't forget

Detailed description of each program in the OpenOffice suite can be found in chapter four.

5 Now launch the OpenOffice Word Processor and Spreadsheet programs from the Applications, Office menu on desktops two and three respectively

6 In the spreadsheet window select the File, New, Drawing menu to launch the OpenOffice Draw program

7 Right-click the Draw window title bar and choose Move to Workspace Right – sending that window to desktop four

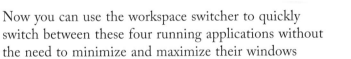

File **Edit**	— Mi<u>n</u>imize	Alt+F9
	Unma<u>x</u>imize	Alt+F5
	<u>M</u>ove	Alt+F7
	<u>R</u>esize	Alt+F8
Ni	Always on <u>T</u>op	
A1	○ <u>A</u>lways on Visible Workspace	
	◉ <u>O</u>nly on This Workspace	
1	Move to Workspace <u>L</u>eft	
2	Move to Workspace <u>R</u>ight	
3	Move to Another <u>W</u>orkspace ▸	
4		
5	✕ <u>C</u>lose	Alt+F4
6		

8 Now you can use the workspace switcher to quickly switch between these four running applications without the need to minimize and maximize their windows

Hot tip

Alternatively you can use the "Move to Another Workspace" menu to nominate a desktop number to move an application to.

Getting help

Help can be sought on applications and any aspect of the desktop from the Gnome Help Browser. For example, you can discover how to configure desktop effects:

1 On the taskbar, click System then "Help and Support" – to launch the Gnome Help Browser

Preferences ▶
Administration ▶
Help and Support
About GNOME
About Ubuntu
Quit...
System

2 From the list of Common Quesitons click the "Enabling desktop effects" item

Ubuntu Help Center

File Edit Go Bookmarks Help

Back   Forward   Help Topics   Search: [   ]

Ubuntu Help Center

Topics

New to Ubuntu?

Adding and Removing Software

Files, Folders and Documents

Customising Your Desktop

Internet

Music, Videos and Photos

Assistive Tools

Keeping Your Computer Safe

Printing, Faxing and Scanning

Advanced Topics

Welcome to the Ubuntu Help Center

To find help, insert a keyword in the search bar

Common Questions

- Connecting to the internet
- Enabling desktop effects
- Playing music
- Importing photos
- Keeping your computer updated

Can't find the answer?

The Ubuntu community provides extensive free support

Canonical, its partners and approved companies provide commercial technical support

How to Contribute

Ubuntu has an open and vibrant community of contributors. Find out how to contribute

3 From the Desktop Effects menu that appears, click on "Configuring Desktop Effects"

Desktop Effects

1. What are Desktop Effects?
2. Configuring Desktop Effects
3. Enable extra Desktop Effects

4 Now follow the Help instructions by clicking System, Preferences, Appearance, Visual Effects, Normal – attempting to enable the standard desktop effects

Normal: Provides improved usability and good balance between attractiveness and moderate performance-requirements.

5 If a password is now requested enter your user password then hit Return to proceed

6 A dialog may now appear advising you that a proprietary driver is needed to enable your graphics card to run desktop effects – if this is acceptable click Enable Driver to download and install the driver

Hot tip
The Help Browser can be launched at any time by presssing the F1 key.

Enable the Driver?

NVIDIA accelerated graphics driver (latest cards)

This driver is required to fully utilise the 3D potential of NVIDIA graphics cards, as well as provide 2D acceleration of newer cards.

If you wish to enable desktop effects, this driver is required.

If this driver is not enabled, you will not be able to enable desktop effects and will not be able to run software that requires 3D acceleration, such as some games.

❌ Cancel   ✔ Enable Driver

7 Restart the computer to allow your graphics card to use the newly installed driver – the windows now launch with 3D effects and their edges have a drop-shadow effect

8 To see even more stunning 3D window effects click System, Preferences, Appearance, Visual Effects, Extra – attempting to enable enhanced desktop effects

Beware
The enhanced desktop effects require a fast graphics card – choose Normal or None on the Visual Effects tab to reduce the effects level.

Extra: Provides more aesthetically pleasing set of effects. Requires faster graphics-card.

41

Summary

- The taskbar and other desktop panels can be dragged from their initial position to any edge of the screen

- The "Add to Panel" dialog can be used to add applets, buttons, launchers, and other items to any panel

- Applications can be launched from the taskbar Applications menu, or from a desktop launcher, or from a panel launcher

- The System, Preferences menu allows many features of the Linux system to be easily customized

- Screen resolution can be changed using the Screen Resolution Preferences dialog

- The Appearance Preferences dialog can be launched from the desktop context menu or from the System, Preferences menu

- Desktop backgrounds can be selected using the Background tab of the Appearance Preferences dialog

- Window features can be customized using the Theme tab of the Appearance Preferences dialog

- The Sound Preferences dialog can be launched from the System, Preferences menu to assign system event sounds

- Volume can be adjusted using the taskbar volume control

- A taskbar Workspace Switcher allows you to quickly switch between applications on multiple virtual desktops

- The Help Browser can be launched from the System, "Help and Support" menu, or by clicking the taskbar Help button

- Assistance for individual applications may also be sought from the Help menu on their toolbar

- 2D and 3D desktop effects can be configured from the Visual Effects tab of the Appearance Preferences dialog but may require proprietary graphics drivers to be installed

3 Touring the filesystem

This chapter describes the Linux filesystem and explains its directory structure.

Meeting the directory tree

When moving from Windows, the new Linux user needs to be aware of some differences between the two operating systems:

● Linux is case-sensitive – Windows is not. For instance, a file named "readme.txt" and "README.txt" are seen as two different files in Linux, but there is no distinction in Windows

● Linux directories and files have ownership permissions that can restrict accessibility to the owner or group – Windows directories and files are generally universally accessible

● Linux was developed from the outset as a multi-user network operating system – Windows evolved from DOS as a single-user operating system intended for home use

● Linux desktop users cannot change system settings, only the "root" Super User may do so – Windows desktop users have free reign to wreak havoc

● Linux partitions are created using the Ext3 filesystem – Windows partitions use FAT, FAT32 or NTFS filesystems

● Linux path names contain forward slash characters – Windows path names contain back slash characters. For instance, a Linux path **/usr/bin** and a Windows path **C:\mysql\bin**

● Linux does not have any drive letters – Windows typically uses C: for the hard disk drive, D: for the CD drive, E: for an external drive, and so on

Hot tip

See page 58 for more on access permissions.

The lack of drive letters in Linux indicates what is, probably, the biggest difference between Linux and Windows – the way their directory structures are arranged. In Linux everything is contained within a single unified hierarchical system – beginning with the "root" directory, symbolized by a single forward slash "/".

The Linux installation creates a number of standard sub-directories within the root directory. Each one of these, in turn, houses its own sub-directory structure, thereby creating a directory "tree" – the "root" directory is the root of the tree.

44

Contents of peripheral drives appear in the tree in the directory at which they are "mounted" by Linux, creating a unified structure.

The illustration below depicts a typical standard directory structure in a Linux file system. All are sub-directories of the basic root directory "/".

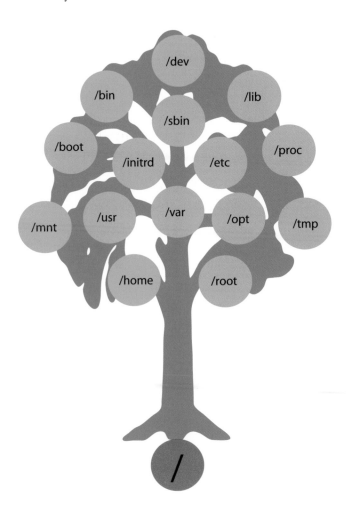

> **Beware**
>
> Do not confuse the /root directory (the home directory of the root superuser) with the / root of the file system.

The purpose of each standard Linux directory is described on the ensuing pages of this chapter.

Recognizing directories

/bin

Contains small executable programs (binaries) which are often considered to be part of the operating system itself – but they aren't really. For instance, when you type the ls command at a prompt, to list the contents of a directory, Linux executes the ls program that is located in the /bin directory. This directory is roughly equivalent to the C:\Windows directory in Windows.

/sbin

Contains executable system programs (binaries) that are only used by the root superuser and by Linux when the system is booting up or performing system recovery operations. For instance, the clock program that maintains the system time when Linux is running is located in the /sbin directory. This directory is roughly equivalent to the C:\Windows\system directory in Windows.

/lib

Contains binary library files which are used by the executable programs in the /bin and /sbin directories. These shared libraries are particularly important for booting the system and executing commands within the root file system. They are roughly equivalent to the DLL libraries in Windows but are not scattered around the system. Having a specific directory for support libraries avoids the common problem in Windows when multiple libraries have been installed and the system becomes confused about which one to use.

/dev

Contains special file system entries which represent devices that are attached to the system. These allow programs access to the device drivers which are essential for the system to function properly – although the actual driver files are located elsewhere. For instance, typically the entry /dev/fd0 represents the floppy drive and the entry /dev/cdrom0 represents the CD drive.

/boot

Contains the Linux kernel – the heart of the operating system. Many people incorrectly use the term "operating system" to refer to the Linux environment but, strictly speaking, the kernel is the operating system. It is the program that controls access to all the hardware devices your computer supports and allows multiple programs to run concurrently and share that hardware. Typically the program is called "vmlinuz" – other programs complementing the kernel are located in the /bin and /sbin directories.

/etc

Contains system configuration files storing information about everything from user passwords and system initialization to screen resolution settings. All these are plain text files that can be viewed in any text editor, such as KEdit – there should never be any binary files in this directory. They control all configuration settings which are not user-specific. The files in this directory are roughly equivalent to the combination of .ini files and the Registry entries found in the Windows operating system.

/proc

Contains special files that relay information to and from the kernel. The hierarchy of "virtual" files within this directory represent the current state of the kernel – allowing applications and users to peer into the kernel's view of the system. For instance, at a command prompt type

more /proc/cpuinfo

to see information about your computer's processor/s. Similarly, typing the command

more /proc/meminfo

reveals information about your system's current memory usage. Unlike binary and text files, most virtual files are listed as zero bytes in size and are time stamped with the current date and time. This reflects the notion that they are constantly updating.

...cont'd

/mnt

Contains sub-directories that act as gateways to temporarily mounted file systems. This is the default location where most distros attach mounted file systems to the Linux directory tree. Typically, when peripheral drives have been mounted, the **/mnt/cdrom** directory lets you access files on a CD-ROM loaded in the CD drive. On systems that dual-boot with Windows, **/mnt/windows** can reveal files on the Windows partition although accessibility can be restricted on NTFS file systems.

/usr

Contains sub-directories storing programs that can be run by any user of that system. For instance, games, word processors and media players. This directory is roughly equivalent to the **C:\Program Files** directory in Windows. The **/usr/local** sub-directory is intended for use by the system administrator, when installing software locally, to prevent it being overwritten when the system software is updated.

/var

Contains variable data files that store information about ongoing system status, particularly logs of system activity. The system administrator (root superuser) can type the following command at a root prompt to see the record of system activity messages:

more /var/log/messages

/home

Contains a sub-directory for each user account to store personal data files. If there is a user account named "fred" there will be a **/home/fred** directory where that user can store personal files – other users cannot save files there. This directory is where you store all your working documents, images and media files and is the rough equivalent of the **My Documents** directory in the Windows operating system.

/tmp

Contains, as you might expect, temporary files that have been created by running programs. Mostly these are deleted when the program gets closed but some do get left behind – periodically these should be deleted. This directory is roughly equivalent to the **C:\Windows\Temp** directory in Windows.

/root

This is the home directory for the root account superuser – for security reasons regular users cannot access this directory. If you login to Linux as root and open that account's home directory it's at **/root**, rather than a sub-directory of **/home** like regular users.

/initrd

Contains only a text file warning that this directory should not be deleted. It is used during the boot process to mount the Linux file system itself. Removing this directory will leave the computer unable to boot Linux – instead it will generate a "kernel panic" error message.

/opt

Contains nothing initially, but this directory provides a special area where large static application software packages can be installed. A package placing files in **/opt** creates a sub-directory bearing the same name as the package. This sub-directory contains files that would otherwise be scattered around the file system, giving the system administrator an easy way to determine the role of each file. For instance, if "example" is the name of a particular software package in the **/opt** directory, then all its files could be placed within sub-directories of the **/opt/example** directory – binaries in **/opt/example/bin**, manual pages in **/opt/example/man**, and so on. The entire application can be easily removed by deleting the **/opt/example** directory – along with all its sub-directories and files.

Navigating with File Browser

The standard Linux sub-directories can be viewed graphically by opening the File Browser application in the / system root location. In Ubuntu, this can be started using the Places button on the taskbar that conveniently lists common locations on its menu.

1 Click the Places button on the taskbar, then choose the Computer menu item to launch the File Browser – showing the system components

2 In the File Browser click on the Filesystem icon to navigate to the / location at the root of the filesystem – showing the standard sub-directories

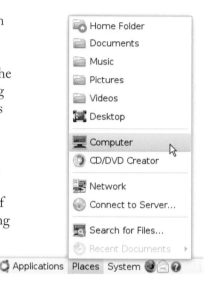

Don't forget

In addition to the standard directories the Ubuntu distro has media, sys, and srv directories – other distros may vary.

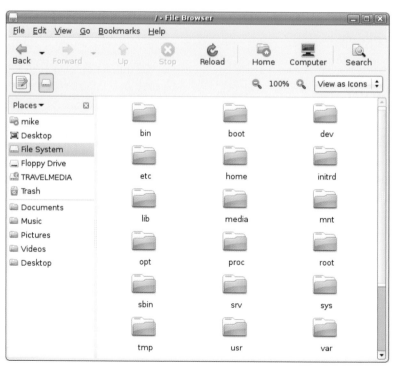

You can navigate through the filesystem in File Browser by clicking on a folder in the right-hand pane, or by clicking on a location in the navigation panel, or by typing a directory address into the location field and hitting the Return key.

3 Click the home icon in the File Browser to navigate to the **/home** directory – there will be a folder there bearing the name of the user created during installation

4 Click on the folder bearing the user name to see the contents of that user's home directory

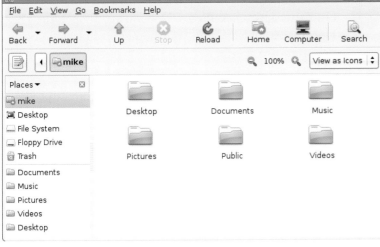

5 On the File Browser toolbar, click the  Up arrow twice to navigate back up to the / root location

6 Click the user's folder in the navigation panel to navigate to their home directory once more, then return to / again

7 On the File Browser toolbar, click the  button to reveal the location field and type the address of the user's home directory (in this case **/home/mike**) then hit Return to navigate to that user's home directory one more time

Hot tip

Notice that File Browser displays the name of the currently displayed directory on its title bar.

Hot tip

The current user's home directory folders can be quickly accessed from the taskbar Places menu.

51

Handling files

All data files you create in Linux should only be saved in your home directory, or its sub-directories. They can be revisited at any time using File Browser and can be easily copied, moved, renamed, or deleted.

 1 Click on Applications, Accessories, Text Editor to launch a plain text editor, then type in some text and click the Save button on the toolbar (or the File, Save menu item)

2 In the Save As dialog select the user's Documents folder and type a name for the text document, say "sample.txt", then click the Save button

3 On the taskbar click Places, Documents to open the Documents folder within your home directory and locate the saved text file

4 Right-click on the file's icon and choose Copy from the context menu – to copy that file to the clipboard

Beware

Directories may contain hidden files – click the View, Show Hidden Files menu in File Browser to also show hidden files.

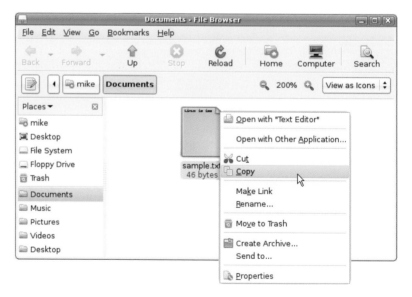

5 Navigate to the Public folder within the user's home directory, then right-click and choose Paste Into Folder from the context menu – to deposit a copy of the file

6 Click open the Public folder then right-click on the copied file and choose Rename from the context menu to see the file name get highlighted – ready to be changed

7 Now type a new file name, say "open.txt", then hit Return to rename the file

8 Right-click on the renamed file and choose "Cut" from the context menu

9 Navigate back to the Documents folder, then right-click on the File Browser window and choose Paste from the context menu – depositing the renamed file

10 Drag the mouse pointer across both files then right-click and choose "Move to Trash" to delete the files

Creating shortcuts

It is often convenient to create desktop shortcuts to the applications and files you access most frequently. Desktop launch shortcuts are created by dragging the icon from the Applications menu onto the desktop. Shortcuts to files, applications, and URL addresses can be created using the Create Launcher dialog:

Hot tip

You can click on the icon button in the Create Launcher dialog to choose a suitable icon for the shortcut.

1 Right-click anywhere on the desktop, then choose Create Launcher from the context menu – to launch the Create Launcher dialog box

🖿 Create **F**older
Create **L**auncher...
🖹 Create **D**ocument ▸
Clean **U**p by Name
✓ **K**eep Aligned
📋 **P**aste
Change Desktop **B**ackground

Image Editor

2 In the Create Launcher dialog enter a shortcut Name and application Command, such as **gimp**, then click OK – a shortcut icon will appear on the desktop that can be clicked to launch that application

Create Launcher

Type: Application

Name: Image Editor

Comma**nd:** gimp   Browse...

Comment:

? **H**elp   ✗ **C**ancel   ⏎ **O**K

sample.txt

3 Open another Create Launcher dialog then change the Type field to "Location" – the Command Field then automatically changes to become a Location field.

4 Enter a Name, then the system address of a file in the Location field, such as **/home/mike/Documents/sample.txt** – a shortcut icon will then appear on the desktop that can be clicked to launch a Text Editor displaying that file

5 Repeat step 3, then enter a shortcut Name and type a URL address in the Location field – a shortcut icon will then appear on the desktop that can be clicked to launch a Web Browser displaying that web page

In Easy Steps Website

Create Launcher	
Type:	Location
Name:	In Easy Steps Website
Location:	http://www.ineasysteps.com Browse...
Comment:	Check out the latest titles
Help	Cancel OK

These shortcuts each store the path to the target application, file, or URL – you can drag'n'drop them into a Text Editor to see the path data.

A shortcut to a local file can also be created as a link, which is merely a reference to the target – dropping a link into a Text Editor will open the target file.

6 Open File Browser in your home directory then right-click on a text file and choose Make Link from the context menu – a shortcut icon now appears in that directory and has an arrow denoting it to be a link

Link to sample.txt

7 Drag the link icon from File Browser and drop it onto the desktop to create a shortcut that can be clicked to launch a Text Editor displaying the target file

Care must be taken to maintain links as changes to the target file, such as renaming or moving it, will leave the links "orphaned" – no longer pointing correctly at the target file.

Shortcuts and links can be deleted in the same way as files.

Locating files

It is important to recognize that many directories in Linux contain hidden sub-directories and hidden files containing configuration data. These are like the "System" files which are hidden by default in the Windows operating system. In Linux the name of each hidden directory and file always begins with a dot.

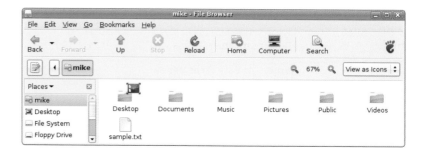

1 Open File Browser in your home directory

2 Click View, Show Hidden Files to see all contents

Hot tip

Right-click on the File Browser window then select Arrange Items from the context menu to choose how contents should be arranged.

The easiest way to find a file on your filesystem is with the "Search for Files" dialog, which can be found on the Places menu. This offers three ways to search for a file – by Name, by Contents, or by Properties.

To speed up the search process you can specify which directory structure to search – otherwise the entire filesystem gets searched. The * wildcard character can often be useful when you want to find all files of a known name regardless of the file extension.

Beware

A search will not normally include hidden files.

3 On the taskbar, click Places, Search for Files to launch the "Search for Files" dialog, then ensure that its "Look in folder" field is set to your home directory

4 In the Search for Files dialog enter a file name, or part of the name and a wildcard, into the "Name contains" field, then click the Find button to execute the search

Don't forget

You can click the arrowed button in the "Look in folder" field to choose a different starting point for the search – choose the Filesystem item if you wish to search the entire system.

6 Files Found - Search for Files				

Name contains: sample*

Look in folder: mike

▽ Select more options

Contains the text: ▭ Remove

Available options: Date modified less than ⊹ Add

Search results: 6 files found

Name	Folder	Size	Type	Date Modified
sample.txt	mike	83 bytes	plain text document	Tuesday, August 14
sample.mp3	mike/Music	3.6 MB	MP3 audio	Thursday, August 16
sample.mpg	mike/Videos	19.9 MB	MPEG video	today at 3:24 PM
sample.jpg	mike/Pictures	64.6 KB	JPEG image	today at 9:57 AM
sample.png	mike/Pictures	555.6 KB	PNG image	today at 9:55 AM
sample.doc	mike/Documents	32.0 KB	Word document	today at 9:55 AM

Help Close Find

Understanding permissions

In Linux each file and directory has an "owner" – generally this is the user who created it. The owner has full permission to read the file, write to the file and to execute the file (if it's executable).

The owner may also set permissions to specify if other users can read, write and execute the file. The file's accessibility can be restricted to the owner, or to a "group" of which the owner is a member, or to any user of the system.

Permission settings of a file can be found on the Permissions tab of its Properties dialog:

 Right-click on a file, then choose the Properties item from the context menu – to launch the Properties dialog

 Click on the Permissions tab to view the current settings

Beware

Checking the option here to allow the file to be executable allows the Owner, Group, and Others to execute it.

---

sample.txt Properties

| Basic | Emblems | Permissions | Open With | Notes |

Owner: mike - Mike McGrath

Access: Read and write

Group: mike

Access: Read-only

Others

Access: Read-only

Execute: ☐ Allow executing file as program

SELinux Context: unknown

Last changed: Mon 27 Aug 2009 01:00:00 PM EDT

Help   Close

Usually the Owner, Group and Others will have permission to at least Read the file. If you are the owner of the file the Owner will have permission to Write – and Execute the file if it's executable.

As the owner of the file you can use the arrowed buttons to modify the access permissions of this file.

 3   Click the arrowed button in the Others field, then choose None to restrict access to the Owner and Group members

Hot tip

When a user account is created a group of the same name is also created – of which that user is a member.

59

---

sample.txt Properties   ☒

| Basic | Emblems | Permissions | Open With | Notes |

Owner: mike - Mike McGrath

Access: Read and write   ⬍

Group: mike   ⬍

Access: Read-only   ⬍

Others

Access: None   ⬍

Execute: ☐ Allow executing file as program

SELinux Context: unknown

Last changed: Mon 27 Aug 2009 01:00:00 PM EDT

   ❓ Help   ☒ Close

Don't forget

If you need to change permissions on files where you are not the owner you need root superuser status – see page 144 for details.

Summary

- The Linux filesystem comprises a number of standard directories arranged hierarchically beneath the / system root

- Data files created by a user should only be stored in the **/home** directory structure – in the user's home directory

- A user can navigate around the filesystem graphically using the File Browser application

- Individual files can be copied, moved, renamed, and deleted with the File Browser

- Desktop launch shortcuts are easily created by dragging an item from the Applications menu onto the desktop

- The Create Launcher dialog can create shortcuts to applications, files, and URL addresses

- A shortcut to a local file can be created as a link, which is merely a reference to the target file

- Care must be taken to avoid orphaning links when the target file gets moved or renamed

- It is important to recognize that many Linux directories contain hidden sub-directories and files

- Hidden files and directories always have names that begin with a . period

- The View, Show Hidden Files menu in File Browser allows all content to be seen – including those normally hidden

- Files can be located quickly using the "Search for Files" dialog to seek files by Name, Content, or Properties

- Specifying a directory structure to search in the "Look in folder" field speeds up the search

- The owner of a file can specify access permissions to allow the Owner, Group, and Others, to Read, Write, and Execute

4 Running office applications

This chapter describes how to accomplish routine office tasks in Linux.

Creating documents

The OpenOffice suite that is included with most Linux distros contains a set of office tools similar to those in Microsoft Office – word processor, spreadsheet, and presentation programs together with a program to create charts, graphs and diagrams, and a specialized database program. If you are familiar with Microsoft Office you will feel instantly at home with the OpenOffice equivalents.

Most importantly, OpenOffice contains file filters that allow it to work with standard Microsoft Office documents from Word, Excel and PowerPoint. Files can be saved in Microsoft Office file formats, as well as formats native to OpenOffice, and objects (OLE objects, plugins, video, applets, charts) can be embedded within a document in much the same way as in Microsoft Word.

62

1. Click Applications, Office, Word Processor to launch OpenOffice Writer with a new blank document open – ready to receive content

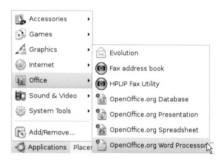

2. Type some content in the new document

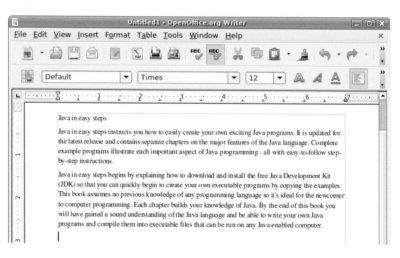

3 Click the Edit, Select All menu item (or press Ctrl+A) to select all content, then choose a font from the dropdown list on the toolbar

4 Select the heading text then use the toolbar buttons to modify the font height, font weight and font color

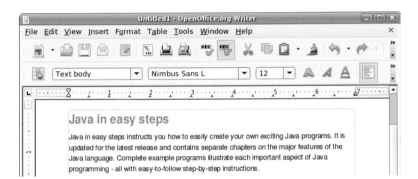

Hot tip

Notice that the text toolbar automatically switches to the graphics toolbar when a graphic is selected.

5 Click the Insert, Picture, From File menu item to launch the Insert Picture dialog, then choose an image file to add to the document at the current cursor position

6 Click on the image and drag it to over the text body, then drop it to see the text automatically wrap around

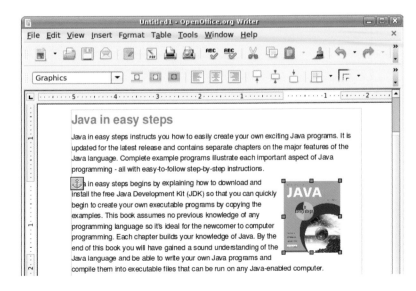

Hot tip

Double-click the graphic to open the Picture dialog where you can adjust the Wrap Spacing distance – and much more.

Exporting documents

When saving documents from the OpenOffice word processor the default file format used is the OpenDocument Text format (.odt). Many alternative file formats are available, however, so your documents can be made compatible with Microsoft Office.

 Click File, Save (or press Ctrl+S) to launch the Save dialog, then type a document name in the Name field

 Click the arrowed File Type button to open a list of possible formats in which to save the document – choose the format named "Microsoft Word 97/2000/XP"

 Choose a location to save to in the Places pane, then click the Save button

Save

Name:	java-book
Save in folder:	🖳 Desktop

▽ Browse for other folders

◀ | 🖳 mike | 🖳 **Desktop** | Create Folder

Places		Name	▾ Modified
🖳 Desktop		📄 java-book.doc	Today at 11:46
⬚ File System			
⬚ Floppy Drive			

➕ Add | ➖ Remove | Microsoft Word 97/2000/XP (.doc) ⬍

▷ File type
☐ Edit filter settings
☐ Save with password

✖ Cancel | 💾 Save

Hot tip

In the Save dialog you don't need to include a file extension in the Name field – it gets added automatically.

 If a warning dialog appears click the Yes button to confirm you wish to save using the .doc file format – the file is then saved at the chosen location

OpenOffice.org 2.3

⚠ This document may contain formatting or content that cannot be saved in the Microsoft Word 97/2000/XP file format. Do you want to save the document in this format anyway?

- Click 'Yes' to save in Microsoft Word 97/2000/XP file format.
- Click 'No' to use the latest OpenDocument file format and be sure all formatting and content is saved correctly.

Yes | No

☐ Do not show this warning again

One real bonus in OpenOffice is the built-in support for the Portable Document Format. This allows you to create read-only versions of your documents in the popular PDF format without any additional costly software. The PDF format maintains the style and content of the original document in a very compact file that can be easily transferred around networks and the Internet.

 Click File, "Export as PDF" to create a PDF version of the document, with the same file name and .pdf extension

6 Copy the documents created in OpenOffice on Linux to a Windows system for comparison

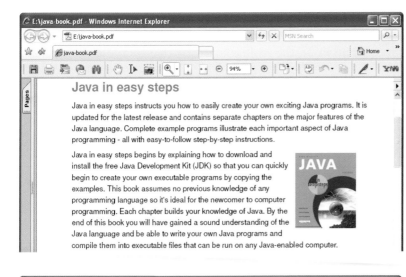

Don't forget

The uneditable PDF version maintains its appearance precisely but the editable DOC version may substitute a different font if the original is not also installed in Windows – more importantly both versions maintain color and layout formatting.

Creating spreadsheets

The spreadsheet program that is part of the free OpenOffice suite provides the powerful ability to perform calculations on data entries using given formulas. It also allows spreadsheets to be saved in the format compatible with Microsoft Excel (.xls).

1 Click Applications, Office, Spreadsheet to launch OpenOffice Calc with a new blank spreadsheet open – ready to receive data

Accessories ▶		
Games ▶		
Graphics ▶	Evolution	
Internet ▶	Fax address book	
Office ▶	HPLIP Fax Utility	
Sound & Video ▶	OpenOffice.org Database	
System Tools ▶	OpenOffice.org Presentation	
Add/Remove...	OpenOffice.org Spreadsheet	
Applications Places	OpenOffice.org Word Processor	

2 Enter some row and column headings then use the color button on the toolbar to accent their purpose

3 Drag over all cells that will contain data then right-click and choose Format Cells from the context menu

Hot tip

You can quickly see a total of all values in a row or column by clicking the gray header buttons – such as the one marked "5".

File Edit View Insert Format Tools Data Window Help

Nimbus Sans L   10

B5:H10   *f(x)* Σ =

	A	B	C	D	E	F	G	H	I
1									
2		School lunch costs							
3									
4		Monday	Tuesday	Wednesday	Thursday	Friday	Total	Average	
5	Week 1								
6	Week 2								
7	Week 3								
8	Week 4								
9	Total								
10	Average								
11									
12									

4 Choose the Currency category in the Format Cells dialog then click the OK button to apply the selection

5 Enter numerical values in all cells for each week row and day column – each value is treated as a currency amount

6 Drag the mouse across each day cell on a row and its Total cell, then click the Σ character on the toolbar – a SUM formula appears in the formula field and a row total value appears in the Total cell

7 Repeat the previous step for each row and column

G9	▼	*f(x)* Σ =	=SUM(G5:G8)				

	A	B	C	D	E	F	G	H
1								
2		School lunch costs						
3								
4		Monday	Tuesday	Wednesday	Thursday	Friday	Total	Average
5	Week 1	$2.70	$2.30	$2.50	$2.65	$2.90	$13.05	
6	Week 2	$2.75	$2.20	$2.40	$2.00	$2.60	$11.95	
7	Week 3	$2.70	$2.70	$2.70	$2.25	$2.35	$12.70	
8	Week 4	$2.70	$2.70	$2.60	$2.70	$2.20	$12.90	
9	Total	$10.85	$9.90	$10.20	$9.60	$10.05	$50.60	
10	Average							

8 Type "=A" in an Average cell at a row end and hit Return, then drag across the day cells on that row and hit Return again – placing the row average in that Average cell

9 Repeat the previous step for each row and column

H10	▼	*f(x)* Σ =	=AVERAGE(B10:F10)				

	A	B	C	D	E	F	G	H
1								
2		School lunch costs						
3								
4		Monday	Tuesday	Wednesday	Thursday	Friday	Total	Average
5	Week 1	$2.70	$2.30	$2.50	$2.65	$2.90	$13.05	$2.61
6	Week 2	$2.75	$2.20	$2.40	$2.00	$2.60	$11.95	$2.39
7	Week 3	$2.70	$2.70	$2.70	$2.25	$2.35	$12.70	$2.54
8	Week 4	$2.70	$2.70	$2.60	$2.70	$2.20	$12.90	$2.58
9	Total	$10.85	$9.90	$10.20	$9.60	$10.05	$50.60	
10	Average	$2.71	$2.48	$2.55	$2.40	$2.51		$2.53

10 Click File, Save (or press Ctrl+S) to launch the Save dialog, then type a spreadsheet name in the Name field

11 Click the arrowed File Type button to open a list of possible formats in which to save the spreadsheet – accept the default .ods format or choose the format named "Microsoft Excel 97/2000/XP" to use the .xls format

Don't forget

You can choose cell colors, fonts, and more in the Format Cells dialog – like the colored cell backgrounds here.

Creating presentations

The presentation program that is part of the free OpenOffice suite provides the ability to easily produce great slide shows. It also allows presentations to be saved in the format compatible with Microsoft PowerPoint (.ppt).

 1 Click Applications, Office, Presentation to launch the Presentation Wizard for the Impress program

2 In the Presentation Wizard dialog, choose to make an "Empty presentation" then click the Next button

3 Select a slide design, such as Subtle Accents, and click the Next button then click the Create button to launch the slide window

4 Click Format, Slide Layout then choose a layout from the selection offered – for instance "Title, 2 Text Blocks"

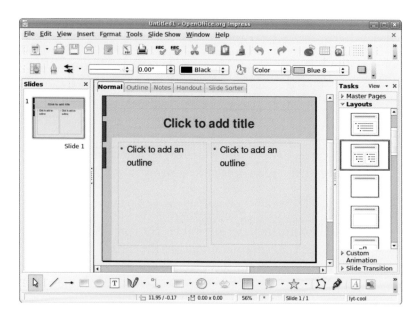

...cont'd

5 Click on the slide where it says "Click to add title" to make the area active, ready to receive content – then type a slide title

Don't forget

Hit Return, or click the mouse button, to advance the slides.

6 Click on the left text block where it says "Click to add outline" then type some narrative text

7 Click on the right text block, then click Insert, Picture, From File to launch the "Insert picture" dialog

8 Choose an appropriate image to add to the slide then use the grab handles around the image to adjust its size so it fits the text block

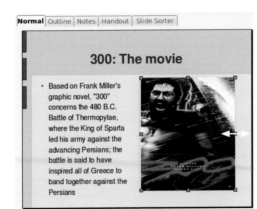

Hot tip

You can click Slide Show, Slide Show Settings then change the type to Auto to make the slides automatically advance at a specified interval.

9 Click Insert, Slide to add more slides, then select Slide 1 in the Slides pane and press F5 to run the presentation

10 Click File, Save (or press Ctrl+S) to launch the Save dialog, then type a presentation name in the Name field

11 Click the arrowed File Type button to open a list of possible formats – accept the default .odp format or choose "Microsoft Powerpoint 97/2000/XP"

Creating charts & graphs

The OpenOffice suite includes an accomplished drawing tool that can be launched from any OpenOffice program to quickly create drawings, charts, diagrams and graphs.

1 From any OpenOffice program click File, New, Drawing to launch the Draw program

2 Click the arrowed button beside the rectangle icon on the object toolbar, then choose the rounded rectangle object from the selection offered

3 Drag the mouse in the drawing area to create a rectangle, then press Ctrl+C,Ctrl+V five times to copy'n'paste, creating five more rectangles on top of each other

4 Drag the rectangles to separate areas, then click the Connector button on the object toolbar

5 Click on a rectangle, then drag to another rectangle to create connection lines

6 Now click the [T] Text button and label each rectangle

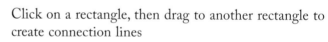

70

7 Click the 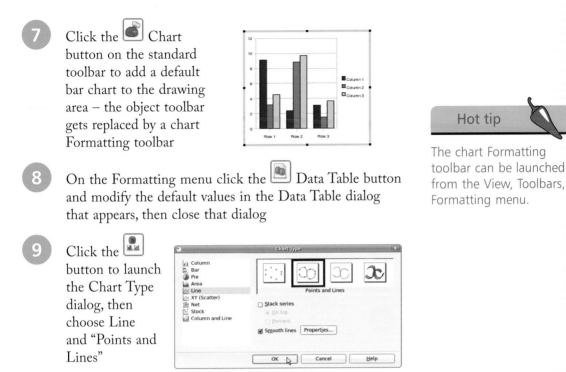 Chart button on the standard toolbar to add a default bar chart to the drawing area – the object toolbar gets replaced by a chart Formatting toolbar

8 On the Formatting menu click the  Data Table button and modify the default values in the Data Table dialog that appears, then close that dialog

9 Click the button to launch the Chart Type dialog, then choose Line and "Points and Lines"

10 Click the OK button to close the Chart Type dialog and apply the chosen line style

Creating databases

The OpenOffice suite includes a useful database program that allows data to be stored in organized tables and selectively retrieved by queries.

Beware

Select the database location carefully as it cannot be easily relocated later – you might usefully create a database folder in your home directory to store all your databases.

1 Click Applications, Office, Database to launch the Database Wizard for the Base program

Accessories ▶	
Games ▶	Evolution
Graphics ▶	Fax address book
Internet ▶	HPLIP Fax Utility
Office ▶	OpenOffice.org Database
Sound & Video ▶	OpenOffice.org Presentation
Add/Remove...	OpenOffice.org Spreadsheet
Applications Places	OpenOffice.org Word Processor

2 In the Database Wizard choose "Create a new database" then click the Next button

3 Now select the options "Yes, register the database for me", "Open the database for editing", and "Create tables using the Table Wizard", then click the Finish button to close the Database Wizard dialog

Do you want the wizard to register the database in OpenOffice.org?

● Yes, register the database for me

○ No, do not register the database

After the database file has been saved, what do you want to do?

☑ Open the database for editing

☑ Create tables using the table wizard

Click 'Finish' to save the database.

<< Back	Next >>	Finish	Cancel

Don't forget

The option to "register" the database only makes it accessible to your OpenOffice suite – it is not registered externally.

4 In the Save dialog that appears choose a location and name for the database, then click the Save button to save the database you have created and to close the Save dialog

5 After a moment the Table Wizard dialog and Project Manager window appear. In the Table Wizard select the Business category and the Employees sample table from the dropdown list

6 From the list of "Available fields" double-click FirstName, LastName, Department, and PhoneNumber to select those fields, then click Next (not Finish just yet)

Category
○ Business   ○ Personal
Sample tables
Employees ⬍

Available fields
Address
BillingRate
Birthdate
City
CountryOrRegion
DateHired
Deductions
DepartmentID

Selected fields
FirstName
LastName
Department
PhoneNumber

< Back   Next >   Finish   Cancel

Hot tip

The Database Wizard can also be launched from any OpenOffice program by selecting the File, New, Database menu.

7 Just click Next again to proceed and choose "Create a primary key", "Automatically add a primary key", and "Auto value", then click Next

8 Accept the suggested table name or enter your own, choose to "Insert data immediately", then click Finish to save the table you have created and to close the Table Wizard dialog

9 After a moment a Table Data window appears with columns for each field you selected in the Table Wizard. Enter name and phone number data for each employee, then click File, Save (or press Ctrl+S) to save the data

Beware

The table ID field will automatically number each row – its value should not be edited manually.

db: Employees

File Edit View Tools Window Help

ID	FirstName	LastName	Department	PhoneNumber
0	Tom	Brown	Workshop	555-1000
1	Andy	Pearson	Workshop	555-2000
2	John	Smith	Workshop	555-3000
3	Susan	Cooper	Workshop	555-4000
4	Debby	Firestone	Workshop	555-5000
5	Les	Barker	Accounts	555-6000
6	Susan	Smith	Accounts	555-7000
7	Jane	Preston	Sales	555-8000
8	Fred	Perry	Sales	555-9000
9	David	Johnson	Shipping	555-0001
10	Susan	Finnigan	Reception	555-0002
<AutoField>				

Record 12   of   12

73

Querying table data

OpenOffice databases can be queried to select data using the Structured Query Language (SQL) or, for those who are not familiar with SQL, a Query Wizard is provided to select data.

 Click Applications, Office, Database, to launch the Database Wizard for the Base program – or click File, Open from any OpenOffice program then select the database

2 In the Database Wizard dialog, choose "Open an existing database file" and choose the database from the previous page in the dropdown list, then click Finish

3 After a moment a Project Manager window opens containing three panes entitled Database, Tasks, and Forms – in the Database pane click the Queries icon

4 In the Tasks pane, double-click the option to "Use Wizard to Create Query..." to launch the Query Wizard

5 The first step in the Query Wizard requires you to select the fields you wish to retrieve from the table. Say you want to retrieve the phone number for Susan in the Accounts department – select FirstName, Department, and PhoneNumber fields, then click "Search conditions" in the Steps pane

6 Set the first search condition Fields dropdown list to Employees.FirstName and type Susan into the Value field

7 To ignore employees with that FirstName in other departments set the second search condition Fields to Employees.Department and Accounts in the Value field

Hot tip

Once created you can double-click a query entry in the Project Manager's Queries pane to run that query again.

Query Wizard

Steps	Select the search conditions
1. Field selection	● Match all of the following
2. Sorting order	○ Match any of the following
3. Search conditions	
4. Detail or summary	Fields / Condition / Value
5. Grouping	Employees.FirstName / is equal to / Susan
6. Grouping conditions	Fields / Condition / Value
7. Aliases	Employees.Departmen / is equal to / Accounts
8. Overview	Fields / Condition / Value
	/ is equal to /

Help   < Back   Next >   Finish   Cancel

8 Click "Overview" in the Steps pane and name the query "Number for Susan from Accounts", then click Finish to run the query

db: Number for Susan from Accounts

File Edit View Tools Window Help

	FirstName	Department	PhoneNumber
▶	Susan	Accounts	555-7000

Record 1   of   1

Hot tip

You can right-click a query entry and choose "Edit in SQL View" from the context menu to refine a query manually.

9 After a moment a window appears displaying the retrieved data and the query entry gets added to the Queries pane in the Project Manager window – double-click the query entry to run the query again

Queries

📧 Number for Susan from Accounts

Sending & reading email

Many Linux distros include the popular Evolution email client application. In Ubuntu it can be launched from a panel icon, or from the Applications, Internet, Evolution Mail menu.

The first time Evolution gets started its Evolution Setup Assistant requests information to establish a default account. Typically you will need to supply the name of your ISP's mail servers (POP and SMTP), and your email address and password. When this is complete, and you have an internet connection, you can start sending and receiving email messages.

1 To check for email messages click the Send/Receive button on Evolution's toolbar, or choose the File, Send/Receive menu, or press the F9 key – the first message you receive is a greeting from the Evolution team

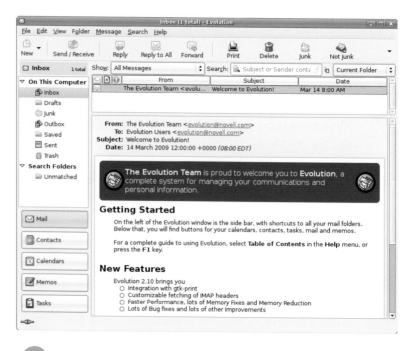

2 To write a message click the New button on the toolbar, then select Mail Message or choose the File, New, Mail Message menu, or press the Ctrl+N keys – a Compose Message window opens where you can type your message

3 In the From field, select the account to send the message

Hot tip

The POP (Post Office Protocol) server handles incoming emails and the SMTP (Simple Mail Transfer Protocol) server handles outgoing emails.

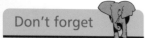

Don't forget

Evolution is also a handy personal manager where you can store contacts, appointments, reminders, and memos.

4 In the Signature field, select the Autogenerated option to automatically add your name to the end of the message

5 In the To field, type the email address your are sending to

6 In the Subject field, type a short message title

7 Now type your message in the main window

8 To add an attachment click the Attach button on the toolbar to launch the Insert Attachment dialog, then navigate to the file and click the Attach button

9 To add emoticons that enhance your message click Insert, Emoticon then choose a meaning from the sub-menu

10 Check the message for spelling errors with the Edit, Check Spelling menu, or press the F7 key

11 To send the message click File, Send, or click the Send button on the toolbar, or press Ctrl+Return

Hot tip

The Edit, Preferences menu in the main Evolution window allows you to edit the email account to your liking – click Add New Signature on its Identity tab to create a custom signature for your messages.

Java in easy steps

File Edit View Insert Format Security

Send | Save Draft | Attach | Undo | Redo | Cut | Copy | Paste

From: Mike McGrath <mike@www.ineasysteps.com>   Signature: Autogenerated

To: readers@example.com

Subject: Java in easy steps

Normal | TT | a | a | a | a | ≡ ≡ ≡ | ≡ ≡ ■

Hi Guys

Thanks for all your positive feedback on my Java book.

It's really fun to program in easy steps. ☺
--
Mike McGrath <mike@www.ineasysteps.com>

▾ Hide Attachment Bar   1 Attachment

java.jpg
(100.0 KB)

Summary

- The OpenOffice suite has filters that allow it to work with documents created by the Microsoft Office suite

- OpenOffice Writer is a word processing program that can create documents compatible with Microsoft Word

- Documents in OpenOffice Writer can embed OLE objects, plugins, video, applets, and charts

- OpenOffice Writer can export documents in the popular Portable Document Format (PDF)

- OpenOffice Calc is a spreadsheet program that can create spreadsheets compatible with Microsoft Excel

- Spreadsheets in OpenOffice Calc can employ formulas to perform automatic calculations using cell data values

- OpenOffice Impress is a presentation program that can create slide shows compatible with Microsoft PowerPoint

- Slides in OpenOffice Impress are created from templates and can employ transition effects and automatic advance timing

- The OpenOffice Draw program can quickly create charts, graphs, and other graphics, in a variety of file formats

- OpenOffice Draw can be launched from the File, New, Drawing menu in any OpenOffice window

- OpenOffice Base is a database program that allows data to be stored in organized tables that may be selectively queried

- Database queries can be made in OpenOffice Base using Structured Query Language (SQL) or by the Query Wizard

- Evolution is an email client program that can send and receive email messages via an Internet Service Provider (ISP)

- In addition to email, Evolution is also a personal manager that can store contacts, appointments, reminders, and memos

5 Running media applications

This chapter describes how to accomplish tasks with various media.

Browsing the web

Most Linux distros include the open-source Mozilla Firefox web browser. This popular free browser is available for various platforms and is highly customizable. It has been developed by the open source community from original Netscape browser source code into a strongly standards-compliant product.

 With an internet connection, in Ubuntu click Applications, Internet, Firefox Web Browser, to launch the web browser

 Type the URL **http://www.babelfish.altavista.com** into the location field then hit Return to open that web page in the browser window

3 Type a phrase in the text area, select a language to translate into, then click the Translate button to translate your phrase

You can click the Use Theme button in the Adds-on dialog to use an installed theme, or the Uninstall button to remove a theme.

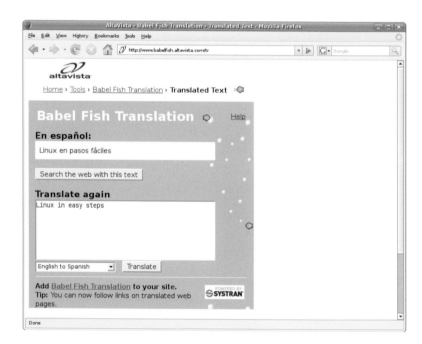

4 To customize the browser's buttons click the Tools, Add-ons menu, choose the Themes icon, then choose Get Themes and install a theme of choice – such as "Blue Ice"

5 Now choose the Extensions icon in the Add-ons dialog and click Get Extensions – from the list that appears search for "Console[2]" and install that extension

6 Click the Edit, Preferences menu then select the Content icon in the Preferences dialog that appears – ensure JavaScript is enabled to execute web page scripts

Beware

Some web pages may not function correctly unless JavaScript is enabled in your browser preferences.

7 Restart Firefox to enable the theme and extension then click Tools, Error Console to launch the Console dialog – this now includes a JavaScript development feature that was added by the Console[2] extension

Hot tip

You can discover how to create your own custom JavaScripts with "JavaScript in easy steps".

8 Type **alert("Hello *your name* ")** into the input field then click Evaluate to see a dialog appear showing your name

Messaging online

Linux distros typically include a cross-platform instant messaging client application named Pidgin that allows you to log in to multiple IM accounts simultaneously. This means you can chat to friends via AIM, ICQ, MSN Messenger, IRC, and many more.

 Click Applications, Internet, Pidgin Internet Messenger to launch the Pidgin application

- Accessories
- Games
- Graphics
- Internet
- Office
- Sound & Video
- Add/Remove...
- Applications Places

- Ekiga Softphone
- Evolution Mail
- Firefox Web Browser
- Mozilla Thunderbird Mail/News
- Pidgin Internet Messenger
- Sun Java 6 Web Start
- Terminal Server Client

2 When the Accounts dialog appears, informing you that no IM accounts are configured, click its Add button

3 In the Add Account dialog, select a Protocol then enter your email address as the Screen Name, and its Password

Add Account

Basic | Advanced

Login Options

Protocol: MSN

Screen name: mike@hotmail.com

Password: ●●●●●●●●

 Click Save to create the IM account and a Buddy List window will appear – click the Buddies, Add Buddy menu to launch the Add Buddy dialog

5 In the Add Buddy dialog select the IM account to chat on, then enter the email address of your friend as the Screen Name and nominate a nickname and group

6 Click the Add button to add your friend's connection details to the buddy list – an item for that friend gets added to the Buddy List window

Beware

Closing the Buddy List window does not close Pidgin – right-click its taskbar icon and choose Quit to close it, or click it to reopen the Buddy List.

7 Double-click a buddy item in the Buddy List window to try to begin conversation

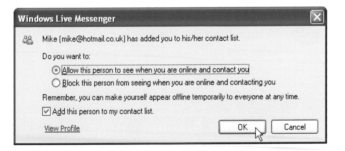

8 On first contact you must both consent to conversation

9 Once consent is agreed a conversation window opens – type your messages in the text field at the bottom of this window then hit Return to send to your friend

Hot tip

Click the Insert button then select an appropriate Smiley icon from the list to enhance your messages.

Phoning over the internet

The Ekiga Softphone application employs SIP (Session Initiation Protocol) to allow free verbal communication via an internet connection – a "SIP phone". It is included in some Linux distros and a version of Ekiga is also available for Windows users.

Each user, regardless of platform, needs to first register a free SIP address which can be used to make phone calls over the internet.

1 Click Applications, Internet, Ekiga Softphone to launch Ekiga – you are greeted by the First Time Configuration Assistant dialog

2 Configuration is a 10-step procedure which you advance by clicking a Forward button. Enter your name when asked then proceed to the important third step

3 With an internet connection, click the hyperlink to **ekiga.net** and complete the form to get a SIP address – enter its username and password in the dialog fields

84

4 Advance through the remaining dialogs accepting the default configuration suggestions, or making changes where necessary – the defaults are usually satisfactory

5 You must register your SIP address before it can be used and Ekiga will have sent you an email for this purpose – open the email and click the hyperlink there to register

You can use the Sound Recorder application on the Sound & Video menu to test a microphone.

6 Connect a microphone to your computer and ensure that it's working

7 Type the SIP address you wish to call into Ekiga's URL field

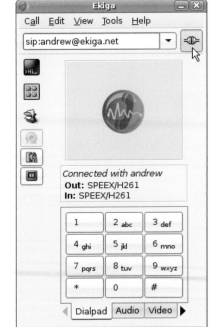

8 Click the ⏻ button or click the Call, Call menu (or press Ctrl+O) to make the call – after a short pause you will hear the ringing tone and the user you are calling will be asked to accept the call

9 Once connected, you can chat normally – call duration is shown dynamically on the status bar

Closing the Ekiga window does not close the application – right-click its taskbar icon and choose Quit to close it, or click it to reopen the Buddy List.

10 When you're finished with the call click the ⏻ button or click the Call, Hangup menu (or press Ctrl+D) – the application disconnects then resumes its Ready state

Watching video

Support for video file playback does vary between Linux distros as most video files use proprietary formats – in contrast to the notion of free software. Consequently the Ubuntu distro does not ship with the codecs needed to play many popular video formats. It does, however, provide an install-on-demand feature that will install the codecs to play proprietary formats if you agree it. This feature starts up automatically when you attempt to play a file of proprietary format in the Totem Movie Player application.

1 Click Applications, Sound & Video, Movie Player to launch a Movie Player window

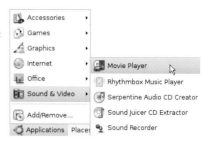

2 In Movie Player select the Movie, Open menu and choose a video file in any proprietary format, such as MPG or WMV. A dialog box will appear offering to search for multimedia codecs packages – click Search

Don't forget

This procedure is necessary at the time of writing to overcome licensing uncertainty – this will hopefully be resolved in the future.

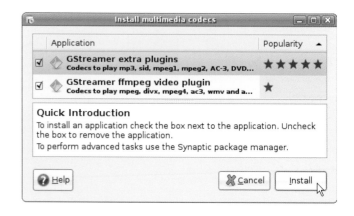

3 In the "Install mutimedia codecs" dialog select both GStreamer packages for installation, then ensure you have an internet connection and click the Install button

4 A dialog now appears requesting confirmation that you are entitled to install the codecs – click the Confirm button if you wish to proceed

The multimedia codecs now download from the internet and get installed on your system. When installation completes support for the proprietary video formats has been added – so Movie Player begins to play your chosen video file.

Hot tip

A "codec" is compressor-decompressor software that processes digital data streams.

Playing music

The Rhythmbox Music Player is great for playing music files and is also a podcast aggregator – and an internet radio tuner.

1 Click Applications, Sound & Video, Rhythmbox Music Player to launch the Rhythmbox application

2 Select Music in the Library window, then right-click on the track window and choose Import Folder from the context menu – choose the Music folder in the Places window to import its contents into Rhythmbox

3 Double-click on any track to start playing that track – when it ends the next track begins to play automatically

4 Select Podcasts in the Library window, right-click on the Feeds window and choose New Podcast Feed to launch the New Podcast Feed dialog – enter a feed URL, such as **http://rss.cnn.com/services/podcasting/newscast/rss.xml**

5 With an internet connection, the podcast downloads from the feed to your computer – on completion, double-click it in the Feeds window to begin playback

6 Select Radio in the Library window and double-click one of the listed radio stations to start listening

	Trollflowers (HBR1.com - I.D.M. Tranceponder)		

Music Edit View Control Help

▷ Play | ◄◄ Previous | ►►I Next | 🔁 Repeat | 🔀 Shuffle | 🔘 Browse | ▣ Visualization | New Internet Radio Station... | 🔊

Trollflowers (HBR1.com - I.D.M. Tranceponder)   2:26

Library ▽	Search:
🎵 Play Queue	🔊 Title	Genre
🎵 Music	HBR1.com - Dream Factory	Ambient
🎙 Podcasts	▷ HBR1.com - I.D.M. Tranceponder	Trance
📻 **Radio**	HBR1.com - Tronic Lounge	House

7 Insert a music CD into the drive bay – Rhythmbox detects it, adding a Devices menu below the Playlists menu

8 After a moment the CD title appears in the Devices menu – double-click the title to begin playing track one

	Bruce Springsteen - Born in the U.S.A.		

Music Edit View Control Help

▷ Play | ◄◄ Previous | ►►I Next | 🔁 Repeat | 🔀 Shuffle | 🔘 Browse | ▣ Visualization | ⏏ Eject | 🔘 Copy to library

Born in the U.S.A. by *Bruce Springsteen* from *Born in the U.S.A.*   1:31 of 4:39

Library ▷	Track	Title	▼	Artist	Time
Playlists ▷	▷ 1	Born in the U.S.A.	...	Bruce Springsteen	4:39
Devices ▽	2	Cover Me	...	Bruce Springsteen	3:28
🔘 **Born in the U.S.A.**	3	Darlington County	...	Bruce Springsteen	4:50
	4	Working on the Highway	...	Bruce Springsteen	3:15
	5	Downbound Train	...	Bruce Springsteen	3:37
	6	I'm on Fire	...	Bruce Springsteen	2:41
	7	No Surrender	...	Bruce Springsteen	4:02
	8	Bobby Jean	...	Bruce Springsteen	3:48
	9	I'm Goin' Down	...	Bruce Springsteen	3:31
	10	Glory Days	...	Bruce Springsteen	4:18
	11	Dancing in the Dark	...	Bruce Springsteen	4:05

12 songs, 46 minutes

Burning disks

Linux distros include applications to easily rip audio files from music CDs and burn files to blank CD/DVDs. Sound Juicer saves the ripped audio files in open source OGG format by default, which can be played by the Rhythmbox Music Player. Serpentine can then burn several ripped OGG files to a blank CD as audio files – creating a compilation CD.

Beware

Not all media players can play OGG files without installing additional plugins – a plugin for Windows Media Player can be downloaded from www.wmplugins.com.

1 Insert a music CD into the drive bay then click Applications, Sound & Video, Sound Juicer – the application recognizes the CD and displays all its tracks

Accessories	▶
Games	▶
Graphics	▶
Internet	▶	Movie Player
Office	▶	Rhythmbox Music Player
Sound & Video	▶	Serpentine Audio CD Creator
Add/Remove...		Sound Juicer CD Extractor
Applications Places		Sound Recorder

2 Check one or more tracks to rip, then click the Extract button – an icon appears against the track being ripped and the OGG file gets written

Sound Juicer

Disc Edit Help

Title: Born in the U.S.A.

Artist: Bruce Springsteen

Genre: Rock

Duration: 46:50

Track	Title	Artist	Duration
☑ 1	Born in the U.S.A.	Bruce Springsteen	4:39
☐ 2	Cover Me	Bruce Springsteen	3:28
☐ 3	Darlington County	Bruce Springsteen	4:50
☐ 4	Working on the Highway	Bruce Springsteen	3:15
☐ 5	Downbound Train	Bruce Springsteen	3:37
☐ 6	I'm on Fire	Bruce Springsteen	2:41
☐ 7	No Surrender	Bruce Springsteen	4:02
☐ 8	Bobby Jean	Bruce Springsteen	3:48

▷ Play   ◎ Extract

Hot tip

By default Sound Juicer saves ripped files in the Music folder within your home directory.

3 Now click Applications, Sound & Video, Serpentine to launch the Serpentine application

4 Use the Add button on Serpentine's toolbar to include ripped tracks in the list of files to write

5 Insert a blank CD into the drive bay then click the "Write to Disc" button on Serpentine's toolbar to start burning the selected OGG files onto the CD – in audio file format

The audio CD gets written with all the selected music tracks and can be played by any audio CD player.

To burn a disc image just right-click on the ISO file and choose Write Disc from the context menu.

Regular data files can be burnt to disk using a special CD/DVD Creator folder, into which files to copy can be pasted or dropped.

6 Click Places, CD/DVD Creator to launch a File Browser window at a special folder location

7 Paste or drop files to be copied into the CD/DVD Creator folder, then click the "Write to Disc" button

In File Browser the CD/DVD Creator folder can be launched from the Go menu.

Creating graphics

The primary image editing application in Linux is the GIMP (GNU Image Manipulation Program) open-source software that includes over 220 plugins in a standard installation. These provide the GIMP with many of the capabilities of Adobe Photoshop but do not provide native support for CMYK colors.

The GIMP is highly configurable and has powerful scripting support but has an unusual appearance, placing the tools in a different window to the image you are working on. GIMP can be used to easily create attractive web page graphics:

1 Click Applications, Graphics, GIMP Image Editor to launch the GIMP tools window, then click its File, New menu to launch the "Create a New Image" dialog box

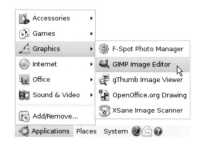

2 In the "Create a New Image" dialog, set Width to 100 px, set Height to 40px, and (under Advanced Options) set Fill With to Transparency – then click OK to launch a new image window with those specifications

3 In the image window click the View, Zoom menu and choose 800%, then drag the corner of the window to enlarge it so the entire image area is visible

4 Choose the ▣ Rectangle Select Tool then drag in the image window from coordinates X:0, Y:0 to X:80,Y:30 – selecting a rectangular area 80px wide and 30 px high

5 In the image window, click the Select, Rounded Rectangle menu – rounding the selection corners to a 50% radius

6 Click each ■ color block in the tools window – set the foreground to #F35F28 and background to #F5D087

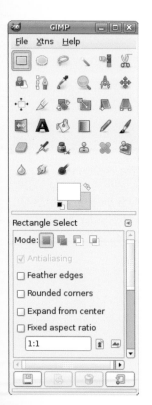

92

...cont'd

7 Choose the 🪣 Bucket Fill Tool, then click inside the selected area in the image window – filling that area with the foreground color

8 In the image window, click the Filters, "Light and Shadow", Drop Shadow menu to launch the Drop Shadow dialog – set both Offsets to 4, Blur radius to 10, Color to the foreground value, Opacity to 80, Resizing off

9 Choose the ▢ Rectangle Select Tool once more and drag from coordinates X:2,Y:2 to X:78,Y:24 to select an area, then click the Select, Rounded Rectangle menu – rounding the corners as before

10 Choose the ▣ Gradient Tool, then drag over the selected area from bottom to top – applying a linear gradient fill of foreground-to-background color

11 Now set the foreground to #FFFFFF, then choose the Text Tool and click on the selected area – type "Web 2.0" in the Text Editor window, then click its Close button

12 In the tools window, adjust the text size to 17, then use the keyboard arrow keys to center the text over the image

13 In the image window, click File, Save and name the image "button.png", then click the Save button – accept the suggestion to Merge Visible Layers during export

14 Right-click on the saved image file icon and choose "Open with Firefox Web Browser" to see how it looks

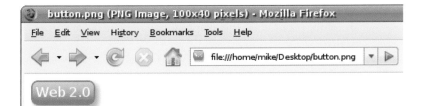

Adding more applications

Linux distros typically bundle the office and media applications most users want, but there are literally thousands more free applications that can be installed with an internet connection.

The Ubuntu desktop makes it really easy to extend your system from the taskbar:

 Click Applications, Add/Remove to launch the Add/Remove Applications dialog

2 Select a category from the left panel, say Graphics – all available graphics programs appear in the top right pane, displaying checked boxes for those already installed

Hot tip

The Add/Remove Applications feature is also known as the Synaptic Package Manager. It is a user-friendly graphic interface for the command-line Advanced Packaging Tool (APT) – see page 146 for more details.

3 Click on any listed application to see a description of that program in the bottom right pane

 Scroll down the list and check the box against a program to mark it for installation, say the Inkscape vector graphics program – the Apply Changes button becomes active

5 Click the Apply Changes button to request installation – a dialog appears allowing the choice to Apply or Cancel

6 Click the Apply button to begin the installation procedure of the chosen application via the internet

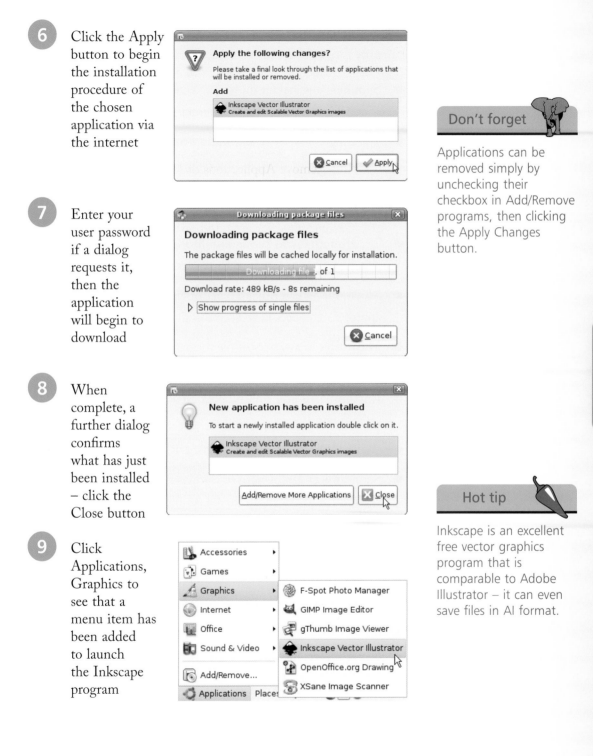

Apply the following changes?

Please take a final look through the list of applications that will be installed or removed.

Add

Inkscape Vector Illustrator
Create and edit Scalable Vector Graphics images

Cancel   Apply

Don't forget

Applications can be removed simply by unchecking their checkbox in Add/Remove programs, then clicking the Apply Changes button.

7 Enter your user password if a dialog requests it, then the application will begin to download

Downloading package files

Downloading package files

The package files will be cached locally for installation.

Downloading file 1 of 1

Download rate: 489 kB/s - 8s remaining

▷ Show progress of single files

Cancel

8 When complete, a further dialog confirms what has just been installed – click the Close button

New application has been installed

To start a newly installed application double click on it.

Inkscape Vector Illustrator
Create and edit Scalable Vector Graphics images

Add/Remove More Applications   Close

Hot tip

Inkscape is an excellent free vector graphics program that is comparable to Adobe Illustrator – it can even save files in AI format.

9 Click Applications, Graphics to see that a menu item has been added to launch the Inkscape program

Accessories ▶
Games ▶
Graphics ▶
Internet ▶
Office ▶
Sound & Video ▶
Add/Remove...
Applications   Places

F-Spot Photo Manager
GIMP Image Editor
gThumb Image Viewer
Inkscape Vector Illustrator
OpenOffice.org Drawing
XSane Image Scanner

Summary

- The Mozilla Firefox web browser is included with most Linux distros and can be easily extended and customized

- Simultaneous instant messaging across multiple IM accounts is possible with the Pidgin Internet Messenger

- The Ekiga Softphone application enables free phone calls to be made across the internet to others who have a SIP address

- Linux distros that only include free open source software will not bundle proprietary codecs for multimedia playback

- The Ubuntu distro has an install-on-demand feature that can install proprietary multimedia codecs when requested

- Movie Player can play all types of video file format when the appropriate codecs have been installed

- Music files in a variety of file formats can be played with the Rhythmbox application

- Rhythmbox is also a useful podcast aggregator and an internet radio tuner

- Audio CDs can be played with the Rhythmbox application

- Sound Juicer can be used to rip files from audio CDs and saved on your system in the OGG file format

- The Serpentine application can burn ripped OGG files onto a blank CD as audio files that can be played on any CD player

- Data files can be burnt on a blank disk using the special CD/DVD Creator folder

- GIMP is the primary image editing software in Linux and can be used to create attractive graphics

- Many additional free applications can be easily added to your Linux system using the Add/Remove Applications feature

6 Commanding the shell

This chapter introduces the Linux shell and demonstrates some basic shell commands.

Invoking the terminal

At the very heart of the Linux operating system is a core series of machine instructions known as the "kernel" – this is a technical program that is not user-friendly as it is mainly designed to communicate with electronic components. A Linux "shell" is a facility that allows the user to communicate directly with the kernel in a human-readable form. It translates command line instructions so they can be processed.

Most Linux distros include several shell programs that offer different features. The default Linux shell program, however, is the Bourne Again SHell (BASH), which is an updated version of the original Bourne shell found in the Unix operating system.

The shell understands a large number of commands and each have a number of "options" that may (optionally) be specified to modify their behavior – usually these are prefixed by a hyphen. Many also accept "arguments" that provide data to be used by the command. The typical syntax of a shell command looks like this:

command -option argument

Shell commands can be executed at a prompt in text interface mode or at a prompt in a terminal window on a graphical desktop interface.

 Launch a shell terminal window (on the Ubuntu desktop, select Applications, Accessories, Terminal)

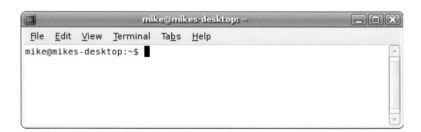

When the terminal shell window is launched it displays the default bash command prompt and places the cursor after the prompt, ready to receive a command. The default prompt comprises the current user name and the host domain name, separated by an "@" character. This also appears on the terminal window's title bar by default.

Beware

Options are not standardized – the same option can have different meanings to different commands.

You can confirm the current user and domain name at any time with the **whoami** and **hostname** commands.

2 Type the **whoami** command at a prompt then hit Return

3 Now type the **hostname** command and hit Return again

Don't forget

Commands use lowercase only – in uppercase the command will not be recognized.

```
mike@mikes-desktop: ~
File  Edit  View  Terminal  Tabs  Help
mike@mikes-desktop:~$ whoami
mike
mike@mikes-desktop:~$ hostname
mikes-desktop
mike@mikes-desktop:~$ █
```

Some commands call upon individual programs that reside on your system – for example, the **clear** command that removes previous content from the terminal. Others are "builtin" commands that are built into the shell itself – for example, the **exit** command that quits the shell and closes the terminal window. You can determine whether a command is a builtin using the **type** command and the command's name as its argument.

4 Type **clear** and hit Return to remove the previous content then enter **type clear** and hit Return again to discover the location of the **clear** command program

5 Now enter **type exit** and hit Return to discover that the **exit** command is a shell builtin instruction

Hot tip

Type a --help argument (two hyphens & "help") after any command, then hit Return, to see a list of options for that command.

```
mike@mikes-desktop: ~
File  Edit  View  Terminal  Tabs  Help
mike@mikes-desktop:~$ type clear
clear is hashed (/usr/bin/clear)
mike@mikes-desktop:~$ type exit
exit is a shell builtin
mike@mikes-desktop:~$ █
```

6 Type the **exit** command and hit Return to quit the shell, closing the shell terminal window

Becoming the superuser

A regular user can call upon many shell commands but some are only available to the privileged root "superuser". These restricted commands typically perform system administration functions to which regular users should not be allowed access in a multi-user environment. For instance, the superuser can use the **reboot** command to immediately restart the system – obviously it would be undesirable to allow regular users access to this command in a multi-user environment.

On a typical home Linux system the user created during installation is given access to the **sudo** command that allows commands to be executed as if they were the superuser. When **sudo** requests a password it requires the user password – not the password of the root superuser.

1. At a shell prompt, enter the command **reboot** to attempt to restart your system

2. As the shell informs you that the **reboot** command can only be accessed by the root superuser enter the command **sudo reboot**

3. Enter your user password, created during installation, then hit Return to immediately restart your system

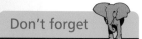
```
                    mike@mikes-desktop: ~                    _ □ ✕
File  Edit  View  Terminal  Tabs  Help
mike@mikes-desktop:~$ reboot
reboot: Need to be root
mike@mikes-desktop:~$ sudo reboot
[sudo] password for mike:█
```

Where the root superuser account is locked by default it can be enabled by providing a password for root with the **passwd** command.

4. At a prompt, enter the command **sudo passwd root** then enter a password of your choice for the root superuser

```
                    mike@mikes-desktop: ~
 File  Edit  View  Terminal  Tabs  Help
mike@mikes-desktop:~$ sudo passwd root
[sudo] password for mike:
Enter new UNIX password:
Retype new UNIX password:
passwd: password updated successfully
mike@mikes-desktop:~$ █
```

Now that the root superuser account is enabled you can login as root using the **su** command with its **-l** option. When a regular user first logs into the shell the working directory is by default that user's home directory. When the superuser logs in with the **su -l** command the working directory is the **/root** directory.

The **pwd** command prints the current working directory and the **logname** command reveals the name of the user who began the shell session.

Hot tip

A user with access to sudo can once again disable an enabled root superuser account with the command
sudo passwd -l root.

5 Enter the **pwd** command to show the current working directory then login as the root superuser and enter the **pwd** command once more to see the new location

6 Use the **logname** command to reveal the name of the user who started the shell session

7 Logout from the root superuser account by entering the **exit** command – to resume regular user status back in the user's home directory

Beware

From a root command prompt you can access any file or program on the system – with the potential to wreak havoc! Only login as root when it's absolutely essential.

```
                    mike@mikes-desktop: ~
 File  Edit  View  Terminal  Tabs  Help
mike@mikes-desktop:~$ pwd
/home/mike
mike@mikes-desktop:~$ su -l
Password:
root@mikes-desktop:~# pwd
/root
root@mikes-desktop:~# logname
mike
root@mikes-desktop:~# exit
logout
mike@mikes-desktop:~$ pwd
/home/mike
mike@mikes-desktop:~$ █
```

Customizing the shell prompt

Whenever a user logs into a shell Linux looks for a hidden configuration file named ".bashrc" that is located in that user's home directory. This file determines the behavior of the shell and may be edited to customize the shell to your preference. It is especially useful to edit this file to customize the appearance of the shell prompt to a style and color of your liking.

 Launch File Browser in your **/home** directory (on the Ubuntu desktop, select Places, Home Folder)

 In File Browser, select View, Show Hidden Files to reveal the hidden files in the **/home** directory

 Right-click on the **.bashrc** file icon then choose Open With Text Editor from the context menu

The **.bashrc** file contains configuration instructions and comments. Commented lines begin with a "#" hash character and this can be used to disable instructions. For instance, the instruction that displays the user name and host domain as the title of the shell terminal window.

 Scroll down the **.bashrc** file to find the line beginning with **PROMPT_COMMAND=** and insert a **#** hash character at the very start of that line

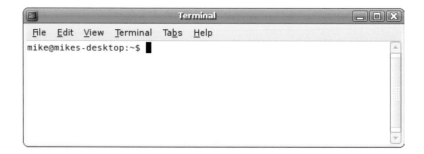 Save the file to implement the change then select Applications, Accessories, Terminal to launch a shell window with a default title bar entitled "Terminal"

102

The appearance of the shell prompt is determined by a shell variable named "PS1", which stores the prompt format. This is assigned a value by the **.bashrc** file to set the appearance and the assignment statement can be edited to change the prompt.

6 Scroll down the **.bashrc** file to find the **case** statement preceded by a comment beginning **# set a fancy prompt** then insert a **#** hash character at the start of each line to comment-out the entire statement – from **case** to **esac**

7 Find the commented-out assignment preceded by a comment beginning **# Comment in the above** and remove the **#** hash character from the line below

8 Save the file to implement the change then select Applications, Accessories, Terminal to launch a shell window with a green colored prompt

```
Terminal                                    _ □ X
File  Edit  View  Terminal  Tabs  Help
mike@mikes-desktop:~$ ▮
```

9 Replace the line creating a green prompt with the line **PS1="\[\033[01;34m\]user> \e[0m"** then save the file and launch a Terminal window with a custom prompt

```
Terminal                                    _ □ X
File  Edit  View  Terminal  Tabs  Help
user> ▮
```

Hot tip

The prompt can be colored black (30m), red (31m), green (32m), yellow (33m), blue (34m) magenta(35m), cyan (36m), or white (37m).

Beware

The assignment statement must be copied exactly as it appears here – without additional spaces.

Changing the run level

The Linux operating system can exist in any one of several numbered "run level" states. Each run level number describes the level of services that have been initialized and are running:

Run level	Description
0	HALT – at this level the system is currently in the process of shutting down
1	SINGLE USER – little more than a single console with almost all other services disabled. Typically used for maintenance, such as recovery from hack attacks or repair of disk corruption
2	BASIC MULTIUSER – most services are running at this level, except for those services that enable network connections
3	FULL MULTIUSER – starts enabled services in text interface mode but doesn't start the X-windows server to run Graphical User Interface desktops
4	USER DEFINED – has no conventional definition but may be custom-configured by the user
5	FULL MULTIUSER GRAPHICAL DESKTOP – starts all enabled services including the X-windows server to run Graphical User Interface desktops. Typically this is the default level for most single-user Linux installations
6	REBOOT – at this run level the system is currently in the process of restarting

Don't forget

Most Linux systems run at level 3 or level 5.

From switching on your system the Linux boot process first starts basic services to attain run level one, then starts further services to continue moving up through successive run levels. Finally, when the Graphical User Interface (GUI) desktop has loaded the operating system is running at run level five.

The boot process calls upon the **init** program to establish each run level and the root superuser can also call this program to switch between different run levels manually. The current run level can be seen at any time using the command **who -r**.

Many Linux systems, such as those operating as web servers, always exist at run level three – without a GUI desktop.

1. Launch a desktop shell window then use the **su** command to login as the root superuser, as described on page 101

2. Enter the command **init 1** to change the run level to the single user Text User Interface (TUI)

3. Wait until asked for a password then enter the root superuser password to get a root prompt

4. At the root prompt enter the command **who -r** to see the run level details

5. Now enter the command **init 5** to return to the GUI desktop at run level five

Hot tip

Notice that the root prompt shown here has been customized by editing the hidden .bashrc file in the /root directory – as described on page 103.

```
Password:
root> who -r
         run-level 1  2009-07-05 14:10                    last=5
root> init 5
```

Issuing the command **init 0** will shutdown the system abruptly. A more friendly shutdown can be achieved using the **shutdown** command with a numeric argument after its **-h** option, specifying the number of future minutes at which time the system will be halted. A system-wide message is broadcast allowing users to complete current tasks before shutdown.

6. At a root prompt, enter the command **shutdown -h +3** to halt the system in three minutes time

Beware

Once the shutdown -h command has been issued the system will halt after the specified delay unless cancelled by root with the command shutdown -c.

```
                        Terminal                    _ □ ✕
 File  Edit  View  Terminal  Tabs  Help
root> shutdown -h +3

Broadcast message from mike@mikes-desktop
        (/dev/pts/0) at 14:22 ...

The system is going down for halt in 3 minutes!
```

Revealing shell variables

Information can be displayed in the shell by the **echo** command. In its simplest form this prints out any arguments supplied to the command. This is not very useful by itself but the **echo** command can also print out values stored on your system in shell "variables".

A shell variable can be created at a prompt in a statement specifying a variable name of your choice, traditionally in uppercase, and assigning a value. Its value can thereafter be retrieved by prefixing the given name with a "$" dollar character.

 1 At a shell prompt, enter the following statement to create a variable named "BODY", storing a numerical value
BODY=98.6

Shell variables can also store text string values but the entire string must be enclosed within quotes in the assignment.

 2 Enter the following statement to create a variable named "SCALE", storing a text string value
SCALE=" degrees Fahrenheit"

3 Now enter the command **echo $BODY** to retrieve the stored numerical value

4 Similarly, enter the command **echo $SCALE** to retrieve the stored text string value

5 Enter the command **echo $BODY $SCALE** to retrieve both stored values together

Don't forget

You can discover more about a command from its Manual page – enter man and the command name as its argument.

```
                          Terminal
 File  Edit  View  Terminal  Tabs  Help
 user> BODY=98.6
 user> SCALE=" degrees Fahrenheit"
 user> echo $BODY
 98.6
 user> echo $SCALE
 degrees Fahrenheit
 user> echo $BODY $SCALE
 98.6 degrees Fahrenheit
 user>
```

Each user-defined variable remains available for recall in the current shell session but can be removed with the **unset** command.

6 Enter the following command to discard both previously defined variables
unset BODY SCALE

A list of standard "environment variables" that store system information can be displayed using the **env** command and their individual values can be seen using the **echo** command.

The most important environment variable is the **$PATH** variable that stores a list of directories in which to seek programs when they are requested. For instance, when you issue a **clear** command the shell consults the value of **$PATH** and looks in each listed directory until it finds the **clear** program – located in **/usr/bin**. Additional directories can be temporarily appended to the **$PATH** list so they will also be included in the search.

7 Enter the command **echo $PATH** to see a list of the standard directories to be searched

8 Now enter a statement to temporarily append a home directory to the list of standard directories
PATH=$PATH:/home/mike

9 Enter the command echo **$PATH** once more, to confirm the home directory has been added to the list

Hot tip

You can append a directory to the PATH each time a shell session starts by adding the statement to the hidden .bashrc file used to customize the prompt on page 102.

107

```
                            Terminal
 File  Edit  View  Terminal  Tabs  Help
user> unset BODY SCALE
user> echo $PATH
/usr/local/sbin:/usr/local/bin:/usr/sbin:/usr/bin:/sbin:/bin:/usr/games
user> PATH=$PATH:/home/mike
user> echo $PATH
/usr/local/sbin:/usr/local/bin:/usr/sbin:/usr/bin:/sbin:/bin:/usr/games:/home/mike
user>
```

Launching apps from the shell

Applications can be launched from a shell window – if you know the correct command for the application. This is not always immediately obvious but can be discovered by examining the application's Properties dialog box.

1 Find a text editor in the Start menu (in Ubuntu select Applications, Accessories, Text Editor) then hold down the left mouse button and drag the item onto the desktop to create a shortcut

Text Editor

	Open
	Cut
	Copy
	Make Link
	Rename...
	Move to the Deleted Items folder
	Stretch Icon
	Restore Icon's Original Size
	Send to...
	Create Archive...
	Properties

2 Right-click on the shortcut and choose Properties from the context menu

3 When the Properties dialog box appears select the Launcher tab to reveal the launch command – in this case it's **gedit** but other editors will have their own command

Text Editor Properties

| Basic | Emblems | Permissions | Notes | Launcher |

Description:

Command: gedit %U

4 In a shell window, type the launch command at the prompt then hit Return to launch the application

Optionally, commands that launch applications from the shell can take an argument to specify the location of a file that application should open upon its launch.

Hot tip

The term %U is not part of the command – it merely signifies that the command can accept a URL as its argument.

5 Select Applications, Sound & Video, Movie Player then, holding down the left mouse button, drag the Movie Player item onto the desktop to create a shortcut

6 Right-click on the shortcut and choose Properties

7 When the Properties dialog box appears select the Launcher tab to reveal the launch command is **totem**

Beware

Never launch an application from the shell when logged in as root unless you are doing so for a particular purpose.

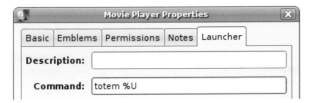

8 In a shell window, enter **totem /home/mike/trailer.mov** (or the path to your own video file) to launch the Movie Player application playing the specified video file

Don't forget

Applications launched from the shell will terminate when the shell session ends – close the shell window to see the application close.

109

Navigating at the prompt

When a user starts a shell session they are, by default, located in their home directory of the Linux file system. The user can switch to any directory to which they have access permission by stating its absolute address as the argument to the **cd** command.

Similarly, the user can return to their home directory by stating its absolute address as the argument to the **cd** command, or using its tilde alias with the command **cd ~**.

For shorter hierarchical moves the command **cd ..** moves up one level to the parent directory of the current directory. Stating just the name of an immediate sub-directory as the argument to the **cd** command moves down one level to that sub-directory.

 Launch a shell window then enter the **pwd** command at the prompt to print the current working directory

 Enter the combined command **cd /etc ; pwd** to switch to the **/etc** directory and confirm it as the working directory

 Next enter the combined command **cd ~ ; pwd** to return to the home directory and confirm the location

4 Enter the combined command **cd .. ; pwd** to switch to the parent directory and confirm the location

5 Now enter the combined command **cd mike ; pwd** to switch to the named sub-directory and confirm it

Beware

There must be space between the command and its argument.

```
Terminal
File  Edit  View  Terminal  Tabs  Help
user> pwd
/home/mike
user> cd /etc ; pwd
/etc
user> cd ~ ; pwd
/home/mike
user> cd .. ; pwd
/home
user> cd mike ; pwd
/home/mike
user>
```

The contents of the current directory can be revealed using the **ls** command to display a list of its files and immediate sub-directories. This is a comprehensive command that has many useful options:

- Use the **-a** option to see all directory contents – including hidden files and hidden sub-directories

- Use the **-l** option to see long format listing for each item – including user and group ownership names

- Use the **-t** option to sort the contents by the time they were created or last modified

- Use the **-o** option to suppress group ownership details

- Use the **-g** option to suppress user ownership details

Options can be combined to produce a complex option where each parameter is applied.

6   Enter the command **cd "My Documents"** to move to an immediate sub-directory whose name contains a space

7   Next enter the **ls** command to simply list all its contents

8   Finally enter the command **ls -altog** to list all contents including hidden files, in long format, listed by modification time – but with user and group details suppressed

Hot tip

Directory names that contain spaces must be enclosed within quotation marks when specified as a command argument – to avoid truncation of the name.

111

Don't forget

All absolute directory addresses begin with a "/" character – as they descend from the / root location.

```
Terminal                                    _ □ X
File  Edit  View  Terminal  Tabs  Help
user> cd "My Documents"
user> ls
linux.txt  My Topics  sample.txt
user> ls -altog
total 20
drwxr-xr-x  3 4096 2009-07-06 16:47 .
drwxr-xr-x  2 4096 2009-07-06 16:46 My Topics
drwxr-xr-x 31 4096 2009-07-06 16:45 ..
-rw-r--r--  1   10 2009-07-06 16:45 linux.txt
-rw-r--r--  1   10 2009-07-06 16:44 sample.txt
user> ▊
```

Operating on directories

It is sometimes useful to be able to extract the name of a file, program, or directory, from the end of a path address using the **basename** command. Conversely you can use the **dirname** command to remove the final part of the path address to a file – leaving just the path to its parent directory.

A new directory can be created in the current working directory by specifying a directory name of your choice as the argument to the **mkdir** command. Alternatively, a new directory can be created elsewhere by specifying a full path as the argument.

Don't forget

The basename and dirname commands simply manipulate the path string – they do not implement any action.

1   To discover the location of the **bash** program that is the default shell, at a prompt enter the command **echo $SHELL**

2   Issue a **basename $SHELL** command to extract the program name from the path address

3   Issue a **dirname $SHELL** command to extract the parent directory of the **bash** program name from the path

4   Enter the command **mkdir Sub1** to create a new directory named "Sub1" in the current working directory

5   Now enter the command **mkdir /home/mike/Folder/Sub2** to create a new directory named "Sub2" using an absolute path address

```
                              Terminal                        _ □ ✕
 File   Edit   View   Terminal   Tabs   Help
user> echo $SHELL
/bin/bash
user> basename $SHELL ; dirname $SHELL
bash
/bin
user> pwd ; ls
/home/mike/Folder
user> mkdir Sub1
user> mkdir /home/mike/Folder/Sub2
user> pwd ; ls
/home/mike/Folder
Sub1  Sub2
user>
```

Directories can be removed in the shell using the **rmdir** command. This takes the directory name as its argument and will instantly remove an empty directory, but will simply warn you that the directory is not empty if it contains files.

Having to delete files manually, one by one, may provide safeguards but can be tedious. An intelligent alternative is available by using the recursive interactive **-ri** option of the **rm** command. This steps inside the directory and examines every file – requesting your confirmation before deleting each file. When all files have been deleted it then asks if you want to delete the directory.

6 Launch the Text Editor using the **gedit** command and create three text files in the "Sub2" directory

7 Issue the command **rmdir Sub1** to remove the empty "Sub1" directory

8 Now issue the command **rmdir Sub2** to attempt to remove the non-empty "Sub2" directory

9 Enter the command **rm -ri Sub2** to interactively delete the files within the "Sub2" directory, and remove the directory itself, by replying "y" (yes) to each question,

```
                         Terminal                    _ □ ✕
File   Edit   View   Terminal   Tabs   Help
user> ls
Sub1   Sub2
user> rmdir Sub1
user> rmdir Sub2
rmdir: Sub2: Directory not empty
user> rm -ri Sub2
rm: descend into directory `Sub2'? y
rm: remove regular file `Sub2/file-1'? y
rm: remove regular file `Sub2/file-3'? y
rm: remove regular file `Sub2/file-2'? y
rm: remove directory `Sub2'? y
user> ls
user> █
```

Hot tip

You can use a -v option with both the rmdir command and the rm command to produce verbose outout – describing what is happening.

Beware

If you're feeling brave, and are absolutely certain that the directory contains nothing you will miss, you can use the rm command with just a -r option to instantly delete a directory and its entire contents – use with care!

Summary

- The **whoami** command states the user name and the **hostname** command states the host domain name

- Previous shell output can be removed using the **clear** command and a shell session terminated with the **exit** command

- A **sudo** command exectues commands as if the user is the root superuser – but you can switch to root using the **su** command

- The **pwd** command displays the current working directory

- Upon starting a shell session the **bash** program reads the user's **.bashrc** file, which can be edited to customize the shell

- The root superuser can change the system run level with the **init** command

- Shell variables exist for the duration of the shell session and their values can be retrieved by prefixing their name with a "$"

- Environment variables, such as **$PATH** store system information

- The Launcher tab of an application's Properties dialog contains the command to launch that application from the shell

- Navigating the file system with the **cd** command can be achieved with both absolute and relative addresses

- The "~" tilde character is an alias for a user's home directory

- Contents of a directory can be viewed in a variety of formats using the available options of the **ls** command

- The **basename** command returns the last part of an address, whereas the **dirname** command returns just the first part

- New directories can be created using the **mkdir** command

- The **rmdir** command will only remove empty directories

- Directories that are not empty can be deleted by the **rm** command, whose **-ri** option requests confirmation before deleting each file

7 Handling files in the shell

This chapter demonstrates how to work with files from a command prompt in the Linux shell.

Managing files

The shell **mv** command lets you easily move files around your Linux system from the command line. This command requires two arguments stating the name of the file to be moved and the destination to which it should be moved.

Interestingly, the **mv** command can also be used to rename a file by stating its current name and a new name as its two arguments.

If you wish to copy, rather than move, a file to a new location the **cp** command can be used. This command can accept one or more files to be copied as its arguments, stating the destination as the final argument.

1 Launch a shell terminal window then enter an **ls** command to see the contents of your home directory

2 Issue a **mv** command to rename an existing file, say from "alpha.txt" to "zebra.txt" with **mv alpha.txt zebra.txt** – and an **ls** command to confirm the name change

3 Enter **mv zebra.txt Docs** to move the renamed file to a **Docs** sub-directory – and an **ls** command to see it's gone

4 Enter **cp some.txt Docs** to copy a file named "some.txt" to the same sub-directory

5 Issue an **ls** command with the name of the sub-directory as an argument to see its contents – confirming one file was moved there and another was copied there

Hot tip

Use the -i option with the mv command to prompt before overwriting a file of the same name.

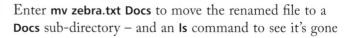

```
                           Terminal
 File   Edit   View   Terminal   Tabs   Help
user> ls
alpha.txt   Desktop   Docs   Pictures   some.txt
user> mv alpha.txt zebra.txt
user> ls
Desktop   Docs   Pictures   some.txt   zebra.txt
user> mv zebra.txt Docs
user> ls
Desktop   Docs   Pictures   some.txt
user> cp some.txt Docs
user> ls Docs
some.txt   zebra.txt
user>
```

The **rm** command can be used to delete one or more files named as its arguments. The * wildcard can also be used to delete all files in a directory – if you are absolutely certain none are needed.

You can create hard links, pointing to the system address of a file, and soft (symbolic) links, storing the path to a file, with the **ln** command. By default this will create a hard link to the file named as its argument – use its **-s** option to create a symbolic link.

The **readlink** command can be used to discover the target to which a symbolic link is pointing.

Beware

The wildcard * character means "all" and should be used with caution.

6   Enter **rm Docs/zebra.txt** to delete a file in a sub-directory and an **ls Docs** command to confirm it's gone

7   Enter **ln Docs/some.txt hardlink** to create a hard link named "hardlink" to a file in the sub-directory

8   Now enter **ln -s Docs/some.txt softlink** command to create a soft link named "softlink" to the same file

9   Enter an **ls** command to see both links have been created in the home directory

10   Enter a **readlink softlink** command to see the target to which the soft link points

```
                          Terminal                    _ □ X
 File  Edit  View  Terminal  Tabs  Help
user> ls
Desktop  Docs  Pictures  some.txt
user> rm Docs/zebra.txt
user> ls Docs
some.txt
user> ln Docs/some.txt hardlink
user> ln -s Docs/some.txt softlink
user> ls
Desktop  Docs  hardlink  Pictures  softlink  some.txt
user> readlink softlink
Docs/some.txt
user>
```

Don't forget

You can find more details on hard links and soft links on page 55.

Examining file properties

The Linux shell provides many commands that can be used to examine attributes of any file. The most comprehensive is the **stat** command that lists every important attribute of the file stated as its argument.

If you just want to discover the file size use the **du** disk usage command with its **-b** option to count the number of bytes.

Use the **wc** word count command to quickly discover how many lines, bytes, and words, a text file contains or assess what type of file it is with the **file** command.

 Enter **stat Docs/some.txt** to discover the attributes of a file named "some.txt" in a **Docs** sub-directory

 Enter **du -b Docs/some.txt** to discover the size of this file in byte units

 Enter **wc Docs/some.txt** to discover that file's line count, byte count, and word count

4 Now enter **file Docs/some.txt** and **file tux** commands to discover the file type of two files

```
┌──────────────────────────── Terminal ──────────────────────┐
│ File  Edit  View  Terminal  Tabs  Help                       │
│ user> stat Docs/some.txt                                     │
│   File: `Docs/some.txt'                                      │
│   Size: 36          Blocks: 8        IO Block: 4096   regular file│
│ Device: 301h/769d       Inode: 3751939     Links: 2          │
│ Access: (0644/-rw-r--r--)  Uid: ( 1000/   mike)  Gid: ( 1000/   mike)│
│ Access: 2009-07-19 11:04:47.000000000 +0100                  │
│ Modify: 2009-07-19 11:04:47.000000000 +0100                  │
│ Change: 2009-07-19 11:04:47.000000000 +0100                  │
│ user> du -b Docs/some.txt                                    │
│ 36      Docs/some.txt                                        │
│ user> wc Docs/some.txt                                       │
│  2  8 36 Docs/some.txt                                       │
│ user> man du                                                 │
│ user> file Docs/some.txt                                     │
│ Docs/some.txt: ASCII text                                    │
│ user> file tux                                               │
│ tux: PNG image data, 1200 x 900, 8-bit/color RGB, non-interlaced│
│ user>                                                        │
└──────────────────────────────────────────────────────────────┘
```

The **touch** command introduces some interesting possibilities as it can change the Last Accessed and Last Modified timestamp attributes of a file. Used alone it simply updates these to the present time but used with a **-d** option it allows you to specify a date in a variety of formats – specify a day number and month number to set the timestamps to midnight on that day of the current year, or specify a complete date including year and time.

Don't forget

Date numbers supplied as an argument to the touch command must be enclosed within quotes.

5 Enter **touch -d "02/21" more.txt** to update the timestamps of a file named "more.txt" to that date in the current year

6 Enter a **stat more.txt** command to confirm the timestamps have been updated

7 Now enter **touch -d "06/15/2012 12:00" more.txt** to update its timestamps to that date and time in the specified year

8 Enter a **stat more.txt** command to confirm the timestamps have been updated once more

```
Terminal

File  Edit  View  Terminal  Tabs  Help
user> touch -d "02/21" more.txt
user> stat more.txt
  File: `more.txt'
  Size: 18           Blocks: 8        IO Block: 4096    regular file
Device: 301h/769d    Inode: 3752125   Links: 1
Access: (0644/-rw-r--r--)  Uid: ( 1000/    mike)   Gid: ( 1000/    mike)
Access: 2009-02-21 00:00:00.000000000 +0000
Modify: 2009-02-21 00:00:00.000000000 +0000
Change: 2009-07-19 12:23:27.000000000 +0100
user> touch -d "06/15/2012 12:00" more.txt
user> stat more.txt
  File: `more.txt'
  Size: 18           Blocks: 8        IO Block: 4096    regular file
Device: 301h/769d    Inode: 3752125   Links: 1
Access: (0644/-rw-r--r--)  Uid: ( 1000/    mike)   Gid: ( 1000/    mike)
Access: 2012-06-15 12:00:00.000000000 +0100
Modify: 2012-06-15 12:00:00.000000000 +0100
Change: 2009-07-19 12:25:49.000000000 +0100
user>
```

Comparing files

The shell provides several ways to compare two files. You can check to see if two files are identical with the **cmp** command. If they are indeed identical the command reports nothing but if they differ it reports the location of the first difference.

Text files can be compared line-by-line with the **comm** command. Its output is slightly unusual as it creates three columns to indicate lines that match in each file:

- Column 1 – lines found in the first file, but not the second

- Column 2 – lines found in the second file, but not the first

- Column 3 – lines found in both files

1. Use a text editor to create a file named **abc.txt**, with three lines "Alpha", "Bravo", and "Charlie", and a file named **acd.txt** with three lines "Alpha", "Charlie" and "Delta" – save the files in your home directory

2. Launch a shell terminal window and enter the command **cmp abc.txt acd.txt** to discover where the first difference occurs betweeen these two files

3. Enter **comm abc.txt acd.txt** to see a line-by-line comparison

```
Terminal                                    _ □ ✕
 File  Edit  View  Terminal  Tabs  Help
user> cmp abc.txt acd.txt
abc.txt acd.txt differ: byte 7, line 2
user> comm abc.txt acd.txt
                Alpha
Beta
                Charlie
        Delta
user>
```

The line "Beta" is unique to the first file, the line "Delta" is unique to the second file, and the lines "Alpha" and "Charlie" are common to both files.

The **diff** command offers an alternative to the **comm** command for comparison of text files. It too compares line by line and it produces a detailed report showing any unique lines. It can also be used to compare two directories to reveal unique files.

Files may also be compared using checksum numbers to verify their integrity. Checksum numbers are often found on internet download pages so the user can ensure that a downloaded file is intact – typically the checksum is made using the md5 algorithm.

The **md5sum** command produces a 32-byte checksum for the file specified as its argument and should exactly match that stated by the originator if the file is indeed intact.

An alternative checksum can be created in much the same way by the **cksum** command. This generates a CRC (Cyclic Redundancy Check) value and includes the file's byte size in the output.

④ Enter a **diff abc.txt acd.txt** command to discover those lines that are unique to each file

⑤ Now enter **md5sum abc.txt** to create a checksum number for that file

⑥ Similarly, enter **cksum abc.txt** to create another checksum number for that file

```
                          Terminal
 File  Edit  View  Terminal  Tabs  Help
user> diff abc.txt acd.txt
2d1
< Beta
3a3
> Delta
user> md5sum abc.txt
713384a9ade9b18020545df4bc7828c6  abc.txt
user> cksum abc.txt
2386744117 19 abc.txt
user>
```

Don't forget

You can enter the command "man diff" to discover more about the diff output from its man page.

Finding files

Locating a file on your system can be achieved from a shell prompt using the **find** command. This is a very powerful command, with over fifty possible options, but it has an unusual syntax. Possibly the one most used looks like this:

find *DirectoryName* **-type f** *FileName*

The directory name specifies the hierarchical starting point from which to begin searching. If you know the file exists somewhere in your home directory structure you could begin searching there (~). Alternatively, you could use the **su -l** command to assume root superuser status then search the entire file system by starting from the top-level root directory (/).

In this case the **-type f** option specifies that the search is for a file – denoted by the letter "f". The **-name** option makes the search by name – seeking the specified file name.

 Enter **find ~ -type f -name some.txt** to seek all files named **some.txt** within your home directory structure

 Assume root superuser status with an **su -l** command, then enter the root password

 From a root prompt, enter **find / -type f -name starburst*** to search the entire file system for any file whose name begins with the string "starburst"

 Issue an **exit** command to return to regular user status

Hot tip

Use the wildcard * with the file name when you know the name but not the extension.

Don't forget

You can recall the last command entered by pressing the up arrow key.

122

```
Terminal                                          _ □ ✕
File  Edit  View  Terminal  Tabs  Help
user> find ~ -type f -name some.txt
/home/mike/some.txt
/home/mike/Docs/some.txt
/home/mike/.Trash/some.txt
user> su
Password:
root> find / -type f -name starburst*
/usr/share/gimp/2.0/scripts/starburst-logo.scm
root> exit
exit
user>
```

By default the **find** command will only report the location of actual files but you can also have it include symbolic links in the report by adding a **-L** option as its very first argument.

5 Enter **find ~ -type f -name some.txt** to seek the actual location of a file named **some.txt**

6 Now repeat the command adding a **-L** option to also report the location of any softlinks to the file

```
Terminal                                    _ □ X
File  Edit  View  Terminal  Tabs  Help
user> find ~ -type f -name some.txt
/home/mike/Docs/some.txt
user> find -L ~ -type f -name some.txt
/home/mike/some.txt
/home/mike/Docs/some.txt
user>
```

In addition to searching for files the **-type** option can specify that the search is for directories – denoted by the letter "d".

When searching deep directory structures, with many sub-directory levels, it is sometimes desirable to limit the depth of search with the **find** command's **-maxdepth** option. This requires an integer argument to specify the number of levels to search.

7 Enter **find /usr -maxdepth 1 -type d** to report only those directories that are direct descendants of the **/usr** directory

```
Terminal                                    _ □ X
File  Edit  View  Terminal  Tabs  Help
user> find /usr -maxdepth 1 -type d
/usr
/usr/X11R6
/usr/lib
/usr/share
/usr/include
/usr/src
/usr/games
/usr/bin
/usr/sbin
/usr/local
user> ▮
```

123

Beware

The /usr directory has many levels – remove the -maxdepth 1 option from the command in step 7 and run the command again to see all directories.

Reading text files

The simplest way to view a text file in the shell is with the **cat** command. Just state one or more files to view as its arguments and it will display their content, concatenating the text together.

Viewing one or two small text files will fit comfortably in a single window so you will see the entire text. Larger files, however, will exceed the space in a single window so you will only see the final part of the text. The solution is to send the text stream to the **less** command via the "|" pipe operator. This means that the text is displayed one screen at a time, starting from the beginning.

 At a shell prompt, enter **cat quote.txt** to display the content of a text file named "quote.txt"

 Enter **cat quote1.txt quote2.txt** to display the content of two text files on standard output, concatenated together

124

```
Terminal                                    _ □ ✕
File  Edit  View  Terminal  Tabs  Help
user> cat quote.txt
I can resist everything except temptation.
user> cat quote1.txt quote2.txt
[ at the New York custom house ]
I have nothing to declare except my genius.

[ a huge fee for an operation was mentioned ]
I suppose I shall have to die beyond my means.
user> cat ballad.txt | less█
```

 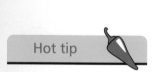
 Now type **cat ballad.txt | less** then hit Return to display the file contents in **less** mode – in which a ":" prompt appears below the content text where you can enter special **less** mode commands to display selective text

```
Terminal                                    _ □ ✕
File  Edit  View  Terminal  Tabs  Help
The Ballad of Reading Gaol by Oscar Wilde

I.
He did not wear his scarlet coat,
For blood and wine are red,
And blood and wine were on his hands
When they found him with the dead,
The poor dead woman whom he loved,
And murdered in her bed.
:█
```

...cont'd

4 Use the Page Up and Page Down keys to scroll through the text in **less** mode

5 Press the > key to skip to the end of the text then hit the Q key to quit **less** mode, returning to a regular prompt

The **head** command lets you preview the first ten lines of a text file and its companion **tail** command lets you preview the final ten lines – great for skipping to the end of a long log file.

You can also display text with added line numbers using the **nl** number line command that provides useful control over numbering. Its **-v** option specifies an integer at which to start numbering and its **-b t** option numbers only non-empty lines.

6 Enter the command **tail ballad.txt** to preview the last ten lines of text within the file

7 Now enter **nl -v 0 -b t ballad.txt | head** to preview the first ten lines of text – numbered starting at zero, and numbering only non-empty lines

```
                              Terminal                    _ □ ✕
 File  Edit  View  Terminal  Tabs  Help
user> tail ballad.txt
Or heave the windy sigh:
The man had killed the thing he loved,
And so he had to die.

And all men kill the thing they love,
By all let this be heard,
Some do it with a bitter look,
Some with a flattering word,
The coward does it with a kiss,
The brave man with a sword!
user> nl -v 0 -b t ballad.txt | head
     0  The Ballad of Reading Gaol by Oscar Wilde

     1  I.
     2  He did not wear his scarlet coat,
     3  For blood and wine are red,
     4  And blood and wine were on his hands
     5  When they found him with the dead,
     6  The poor dead woman whom he loved,
     7  And murdered in her bed.
     8  He walked amongst the Trial Men
user>
```

125

Don't forget

The shell pipeline technique allows the output from any command to be redirected as input for another command.

Creating & editing text files

The classic Linux shell program for creating and editing text files is the compact **vi** application that is also found on Unix systems.

 Type **vi** at a shell prompt then hit Return to open the text editor in the shell window

```
                              Terminal                          _ □ X
 File   Edit   View   Terminal   Tabs   Help
█
 ~
 ~                      VIM - Vi IMproved
 ~
 ~            type  :q<Enter>               to exit
 ~            type  :help<Enter>   or  <F1>  for on-line help
 ~            type  :help version7<Enter>   for version info
 ~
 ~
```

The **vi** editor displays a tilde character at the beginning of each empty line. You cannot enter any text initially as **vi** opens in "command mode" where it will attempt to interpret anything you type as an instruction.

 Press the Insert key to change to "insert mode" where text can be input

 In insert mode, type some text into the **vi** editor – the splash screen information disappears as you begin typing

Beware

The vi editor does not have automatic word wrap at line ends – it will wrap mid-word unless you hit Return to wrap a word manually.

```
                              Terminal                          _ □ X
 File   Edit   View   Terminal   Tabs   Help
This is some simple text that is being written
using the vi text editor in a Linux shell.█
 ~
 ~
 ~
 ~
 ~
 ~
```

There are a number of special key combinations listed in the **vi** man pages that let you navigate to different locations in the text but most recent Linux distros use the enhanced **vim** version that let you use the arrow keys on your keyboard for this purpose.

4   To save your text as a file, first hit the Esc key to exit "insert mode", switching **vi** to "command mode"

5   Type a ":" colon to begin a **vi** command – a colon character appears at the bottom left corner of the editor.

6   Now type a lowercase "w" (for "write") followed by a space and a name for the text file, say **simple.txt**

7   Hit the Return key to write the file – in your home directory by default

8   Type a ":q" **vi** command then hit Return to close **vi** and return to a regular shell prompt.

Hot tip

Using vi needs a little practice. Some distros, such as Ubuntu, ship with other text editors – try typing "nano" at a prompt to launch an alternative text editor.

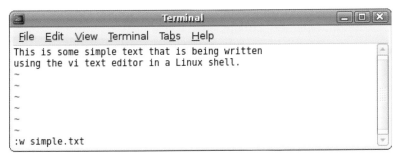

```
┌─────────────────────── Terminal ───────────────[_][□][X]─┐
│ File  Edit  View  Terminal  Tabs  Help                    │
│ This is some simple text that is being written            │
│ using the vi text editor in a Linux shell.                │
│ ~                                                         │
│ ~                                                         │
│ ~                                                         │
│ ~                                                         │
│ ~                                                         │
│ :w simple.txt                                             │
└──────────────────────────────────────────────────────────┘
```

You can launch **vi** and open a file for editing in one single action by typing "vi" at a prompt, followed by a space and the file name.

9   At a shell prompt, enter the command **vi simple.txt** to re-open the text file in the **vi** editor

Don't forget

To edit a file opened in vi you need to first hit the Insert key to enter insert mode.

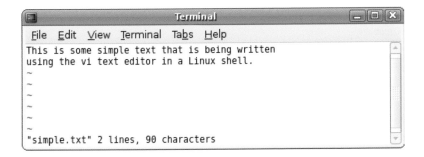

```
┌─────────────────────── Terminal ───────────────[_][□][X]─┐
│ File  Edit  View  Terminal  Tabs  Help                    │
│ This is some simple text that is being written            │
│ using the vi text editor in a Linux shell.                │
│ ~                                                         │
│ ~                                                         │
│ ~                                                         │
│ ~                                                         │
│ ~                                                         │
│ "simple.txt" 2 lines, 90 characters                       │
└──────────────────────────────────────────────────────────┘
```

Manipulating text content

The shell **cut** and **paste** commands may not be what you might expect. They are used to work with text arranged in columns, delimited by an invisible tab character. Each column of text is known as a "field" and the **cut** command can specify an option to determine which field to display – for instance, the option **-f3** chooses the third column from the left.

The **paste** command is the opposite of the **cut** command, combining columns from multiple files for display horizontally.

 Create two text files named "nums.txt" and "veg.txt", each with two columns of text, separated by tab characters

 Enter **cat nums.txt veg.txt** to display the file contents vertically, one above the other

3 Now enter **paste nums.txt veg.txt** to display the file contents horizontally, side by side

4 Enter **cut -f2 veg.txt** to just display the contents from the second column of one file

128

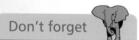

```
                             Terminal
 File  Edit  View  Terminal  Tabs  Help
user> cat nums.txt veg.txt
One     Four
Two     Five
Three   Six
Tomato  Cucumber
Lettuce Onion
Cabbage Cauliflower
user> paste nums.txt veg.txt
One     Four    Tomato  Cucumber
Two     Five    Lettuce Onion
Three   Six     Cabbage Cauliflower
user> cut -f2 veg.txt
Cucumber
Onion
Cauliflower
user>
```

Simple text transformations can easily be made by piping a text stream to the **tr** command. This requires two arguments to specify what to change, and how it should be changed. For instance, the command **tr a "*"** changes all occurences of the letter "a", replacing each one with an asterisk on standard output. Typically the **tr** command is used to transform capitalization on output.

The **sort** command is often useful at the end of a pipeline to display lines of text sorted alphabetically. It can also be used to order lines numerically if a **-n** option is used.

The **tee** command is often used in a pipeline that ends with a **sort** instruction to write the text stream as a file before it gets rearranged. The file name is specified by the argument to the **tee** command and is created in the current directory.

5 Enter **cat quote.txt ; cat quote.txt | tr "a-z" "A-Z"** to display the contents of a file named "quote.txt" – both in its original format and after transformation to uppercase

6 Enter **cut -f2 veg.txt | sort** to just display the contents of a second column, sorted alphabetically

7 Now enter **cut -f2 veg.txt | veg-col2.txt | sort** to save a second column as a text file before displaying it sorted alphabetically on standard output

8 Finally enter **cat veg-col2.txt** to display the saved column

129

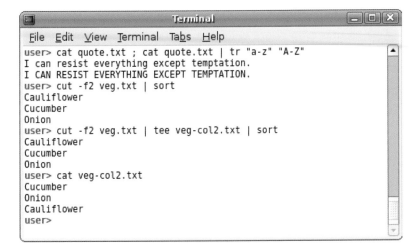

```
Terminal
File  Edit  View  Terminal  Tabs  Help
user> cat quote.txt ; cat quote.txt | tr "a-z" "A-Z"
I can resist everything except temptation.
I CAN RESIST EVERYTHING EXCEPT TEMPTATION.
user> cut -f2 veg.txt | sort
Cauliflower
Cucumber
Onion
user> cut -f2 veg.txt | tee veg-col2.txt | sort
Cauliflower
Cucumber
Onion
user> cat veg-col2.txt
Cucumber
Onion
Cauliflower
user>
```

Matching text patterns

The **grep** command is one of the most useful of all commands. It has many possible options but its purpose is simply to display all lines from a text file that contain a specified string or pattern. A simple **grep** command can specify a string to seek as its first argument and the file name as its second argument.

 At a shell prompt, enter **grep sword ballad.txt** to display all lines in this text file that contain the word "sword"

```
Terminal                                        _  □  X
File  Edit  View  Terminal  Tabs  Help
user> grep sword ballad.txt
The brave man with a sword!
For, right within, the sword of Sin
The brave man with a sword!
user>
```

Notice that the output above has two duplicate lines. The **sort** command can be used to re-order lines, to make duplicate lines appear in succession, and duplicated successive lines can be removed with the **uniq** command. This means that the output from the **grep** command can be piped to a **sort** command to make the duplicate lines successive, then piped to **uniq** so only unique lines remain.

 Enter **grep sword ballad.txt | sort | uniq** to display all unique lines in this text file that contain the word "sword"

```
Terminal                                        _  □  X
File  Edit  View  Terminal  Tabs  Help
user> grep sword ballad.txt | sort | uniq
For, right within, the sword of Sin
The brave man with a sword!
user> ▊
```

Hot tip

The grep command can also match regular expressions. For instance, grep [Y] ballad.txt would output all lines that have an uppercase Y. See the grep man page for more on regular expressions.

The **look** command is useful to quickly output all lines of text from a file that begin with a specified prefix.

 Enter **look Y ballad.txt** to see a list of lines beginning with the letter "Y" from this text file

```
                          Terminal                        _ □ X
File  Edit  View  Terminal  Tabs  Help
user> look Y ballad.txt
Yet each man kills the thing he loves
Yet each man does not die.
Yet though the hideous prison-wall
Yet all is well; he has but passed
user>
```

Hot tip

You can also use the look command with a string argument to see a list of words starting with that string – taken from an editable dictionary file that is normally located at /usr/share/dict/words.

The **aspell** program is a powerful spell-checker that has a **-c** option that lets you interactively check a file for spelling errors. This highlights possible errors and suggests alternatives that you can choose to replace, or ignore, each highlighted word in turn.

 Enter **aspell ballad.txt** to begin the spell-checker for this text file

5 Type the number against a suggested replacement to immediately replace the highlighted word with it

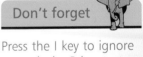
Don't forget

Press the I key to ignore a word, the R key to type your own replacement, or the X key to exit the aspell spell-checker.

```
                          Terminal                        _ □ X
File  Edit  View  Terminal  Tabs  Help
Dear Christ! the very prison walls
Suddenly seemed to reel,
And the sky above my head became
Like a casque of scorching steel;
And, though I was a soul in pain,
My pain I could not feel.

1) cask            6) claque
2) Basque          7) Case
3) basque          8) case
4) masque          9) Cassie
5) Casie           0) caste
i) Ignore          I) Ignore all
r) Replace         R) Replace all
a) Add             l) Add Lower
b) Abort           x) Exit

?
```

Summary

- Files can be moved or renamed with the **mv** command, copied with the **cp** command, and deleted with the **rm** command

- Hard links and soft links can be created with the **ln** command but the **readlink** command can only be used with soft links

- The **stat** command lists all file properties, the **du** command reports the file size, and the **file** command displays the file type

- Timestamps of a file can be modified with the **touch** command and the **wc** command reports the word count of a text file

- Files can be compared with **cmp**, **comm**, and **diff** commands

- Checksums are generated by **cksum** and **md5sum** commands

- The **find** command is used to locate a file on the Linux system

- Contents of one or more text files can be viewed using the **cat** command and lines numbered by the **nl** command

- The **less** command allows lengthy text files to be viewed one screen at a time and can move both back and forward

- While the **head** command displays the first ten lines of a file the **tail** command displays the final ten lines

- The **vi** text editor is used to create and edit text files in the shell

- Individual columns can be selected by the **cut** command and combined on standard output by the **paste** command

- A shell pipeline redirects output from one command to be used as input for another command and often includes a **tee** command to also write output to a file

- Output can be transformed by the **tr** command and sorted alphabetically or numerically using the **sort** command

- The **grep** command searches text files for a specified string and the **look** command can find lines starting with a given letter

- Spelling can be checked for errors with the **aspell** command

8 Performing shell operations

This chapter demonstrates how to execute many routine tasks in the Linux shell.

Handling archives

The traditional GNU zip file compression tool in Linux uses the **gzip** command to compact one or more files, stated as its arguments, into a single archive – adding a ".gz" file extension and replacing the original files. Conversely, its companion **gunzip** command can be used to extract files from an archive created with **gzip** – replacing the compressed archive.

 At a shell prompt, issue a command **du -b ele*** to learn the byte size of any local files whose names begin "ele" – in this example there's just one, named **elegy.txt**

 Enter **gzip elegy.txt** to create a compressed archive of that file – named with an added ".gz" file extension

 Use a further **du -b ele*** command to compare the file size of the compressed **gzip** archive to the original file

4 Enter **gunzip elegy.txt.gz** to extract the original file – being sure to include the added ".gz" file extension

```
Terminal
File  Edit  View  Terminal  Tabs  Help
user> du -b ele*
5699    elegy.txt
user> gzip elegy.txt
user> du -b ele*
2982    elegy.txt.gz
user> gunzip elegy.txt.gz
user>
```

Don't forget

A bzip2 archive file size is smaller than gzip and zip archives – notice the size of the archives in these examples.

The more modern **bzip2** compression tool achieves better compression than **gzip** but is less widely used – distributing **bzip2** archives may not find universal acceptance. It works just like the **gzip** tool, but adding a ".bz2" file extension, and also has a companion **bunzip2** uncompressor.

5 Issue a command **du -b ele*** to learn the byte size of any local files whose names begin "ele" – in this example there's just one, named **elegy.txt**

 Enter **bzip2 elegy.txt** to create a compressed archive of that file – named with an added ".bz2" file extension

...cont'd

7 Use a further **du -b ele*** command to compare the file size of the compressed **bzip2** archive to the original file

8 Enter **bunzip2 elegy.txt.bz2** to extract the original file – being sure to include the added ".bz2" file extension

```
user> du -b ele*
5699     elegy.txt
user> bzip2 elegy.txt
user> du -b ele*
2755     elegy.txt.bz2
user> bunzip2 elegy.txt.bz2
user> █
```

Compressed archives created on Windows systems invariably use the zip compression format. Their contents can be extracted in Linux by the **unzip** command and archives created in Linux for distribution to Windows users with the **zip** command. Unlike **gunzip** and **bunzip2**, the **unzip** command does not delete the archive file after extraction.

9 Enter **zip elegy.zip elegy.txt** to specify the archive name and the file it should contain in compressed form

10 Issue another **du -b ele*** command to compare file sizes

11 Enter **unzip elegy.zip** to extract the zip archive contents

12 When asked, choose the "r" option, then rename the extracted file **elegy-unzipped** – to differ from the original

```
user> zip elegy.zip elegy.txt
  adding: elegy.txt (deflated 48%)
user> du -b ele*
5699     elegy.txt
3104     elegy.zip
user> unzip elegy.zip
Archive:  elegy.zip
replace elegy.txt? [y]es, [n]o, [A]ll, [N]one, [r]ename: r
new name: elegy-unzipped█
```

Beware

The zip command requires the archive name as its first argument, followed by a list of files to be included in that archive.

135

Hot tip

Use a -c option with gunzip, bunzip2, or unzip commands to display the content of compressed text files on standard oputput.

Making backups

Linux provides many tools to archive your data and backup your system onto a tape drive, CD, remote machine or other location.

The **cpio** command can be used to copy output to an archive, or copy input from an archive. It must always employ either a **-i** input option or a **-o** output option to specify the direction of data flow. An output data stream from **cpio** can be sent to an archive file using the **>** redirection operator. Similarly, an input stream can be retrieved from an archive using the **<** operator.

Beware

The user needs to have access permission to the backup location. If this is not granted use the **su** command to assume root status before making the backup.

 1 Issue an **ls** command to list the current directory files

 2 Pipe all files to **cpio** for output to a backup location on a different **ls | cpio -o > /dev/hda5**

3 Enter **rm * ; ls** to delete all files in the current directory and to confirm it is now empty

4 Restore all files by input from the backup location with the command **cpio -i < /dev/hda5**

5 Issue another **ls** command to confirm the files are restored

```
Terminal                                    _ □ ✕

File  Edit  View  Terminal  Tabs  Help
user> ls
document.doc  picture.png  spreadsheet.xls
photo.jpg     plain.txt    video.mpg
user> ls | cpio -o > /dev/hda5
1290 blocks
user> rm * ; ls
user> cpio -i < /dev/hda5
1290 blocks
user> ls
document.doc  picture.png  spreadsheet.xls
photo.jpg     plain.txt    video.mpg
user> ▮
```

Hot tip

Arguably **tar** is less efficient than the **cpio** command but it offers simpler syntax and is widely used – the choice is largely a matter of personal preference.

The **tar** tape archive command is an alternative backup facility with a **-cf** option to create files and an **-xf** option to extract files.

 6 Issue an **ls** command to list the current directory files, then backup all files to a different drive partition with the command **tar -cf /dev/hda5 ***

7 Enter **rm * ; ls** to delete all files in the current directory and to confirm it is now empty

8 Restore all files by extracting from the backup location with the command **tar -xf /dev/hda5**

9 Issue another **ls** command to confirm the files are restored

```
                          Terminal                    _ □ ✕
 File  Edit  View  Terminal  Tabs  Help
user> ls
document.doc  picture.png  spreadsheet.xls
photo.jpg     plain.txt    video.mpg
user> tar -cf /dev/hda5 *
user> rm * ; ls
user> tar -xf /dev/hda5
user> ls
document.doc  picture.png  spreadsheet.xls
photo.jpg     plain.txt    video.mpg
user>
```

The **tar** command can also incorporate a **-z** option that calls upon **gzip** and **gunzip** to work with compressed "tarball" archives.

10 Enter the command **tar -czf backup.tar.gz *** to create a tarball archive of all files in the current directory

11 Move the tarball to a different directory then extract all archived files with the command **tar -xzf backup.tar.gz**

12 Use **ls** again to confirm the files have been extracted

```
                          Terminal                    _ □ ✕
 File  Edit  View  Terminal  Tabs  Help
user> tar -czf backup.tar.gz *
user> mv backup.tar.gz ../Sub
user> cd ../Sub
user> tar -xzf backup.tar.gz
user> ls
backup.tar.gz  photo.jpg    plain.txt       video.mpg
document.doc   picture.png  spreadsheet.xls
user>
```

Examining filesystems

A Linux system may span multiple hard disk drives and extend across many disk partitions. Each partition is represented by a special file in the **/dev** directory – typically **/dev/hda1** represents the first partition on your master hard disk drive.

During the installation process, operating systems format each partition by writing a "filesystem" onto them in which files can be stored and recalled. Similarly, media disks are formatted with their own filesystems to store data. The **df** disk free command shows how filesystems are being used, by indicating free space. It provides a **-h** option to make the output more understandable and a **-T** option to display the filesystem types.

 1   Insert any disk in the CD/DVD drive and close the bay

2   At a shell prompt, enter the command **df -hT** to discover how the filesystem is currently being used

```
Terminal                                    _ □ ✕
File  Edit  View  Terminal  Tabs  Help
user> df -hT
Filesystem Type    Size Used Avail Use% Mounted on
/dev/hda1    ext3   8.4G  2.1G  5.9G  27% /
varrun       tmpfs  252M  112K  252M   1% /var/run
varlock      tmpfs  252M     0  252M   0% /var/lock
udev         tmpfs  252M   76K  252M   1% /dev
devshm       tmpfs  252M     0  252M   0% /dev/shm
lrm          tmpfs  252M   34M  219M  14% /lib/modules/2.6.22-9
/dev/hda2    ext3    29G  182M   27G   1% /home
/dev/hdc   iso9660  697M  697M     0 100% /media/cdrom0
user>
```

The hard drive filesystems on **/dev/hda1** and **/dev/hda2** get automatically mounted onto the Linux file tree during the boot process – to be readily available. The media drive filesystem **/dev/hdc** gets automatically mounted when a disk is inserted into the drive bay. Alternatively, it can be mounted manually with the command **mount /dev/hdc** and unmounted with **umount /dev/hdc**.

Typically, a description of how filesystems are usually mounted, and with what options, can be found in the file **/etc/fstab**. Where a description contains the **user** option (such as the description **/dev/hdc udf,iso9660 user,noauto**) its filesystem can be mounted or unmounted manually by any user. Other filesystems can only be mounted and unmounted manually by the root superuser.

One of the main reasons to unmount a filesystem is to perform maintenance on it without fear of file corruption. For instance, the root user can run the **fsck** filesystem check command to check for integrity and errors. This is the same filesystem checker that is used during the boot process prior to the mount procedures – it should not be used on mounted devices.

The **df** command has a **-t** option that lists only the filesystems of the type specified as its argument. For example, the default filesystem of many Linux distros named "ext3".

3   Use **su** to assume superuser status, then issue the command **init 1** to take the system down for maintenance

4   Enter the command **df -ht ext3** to see just the hard drive filesystems

5   Now enter **umount /dev/hda2** to unmount the filesystem on the partition containing the **/home** directories

6   Issue the command **fsck /dev/hda2** to check that filesystem for errors

7   Mount the filesystem once more using the command **mount /dev/hda2**

8   Enter the command **init 5** to resume the GUI desktop

```
root> who -r
        run-level 1  2009-08-11 11:18                  last=5
root> df -ht ext3
Filesystem              Size Used Avail Use% Mounted on
/dev/hda1               8.4G 2.1G  5.9G  27% /
/dev/hda2                29G 182M   27G   1% /home
root> umount /dev/hda2
root> fsck /dev/hda2
fsck 1.40.2 (12-Jul-2007)
e2fsck 1.40.2 (12-Jul-2007)
/dev/hda2: clean, 429/3784704 files, 165127/7566615 blocks
root> mount /dev/hda2
root> init 5
```

Controlling processes

Your Linux system has many processes running at any given time representing open applications, shell jobs, and background services. Each process has a unique Process IDentity (PID) number. You can see a list of all current processes with the **ps** command and its **-e** option, or see those for any particular user with its **-u** option and the user name. Additionally a **-H** modifier can be used to show the process hierarchy. The process owner, and the root superuser, can terminate a process by stating its PID as the argument to a **kill** command.

Don't forget

Each PID is dynamically allocated by the operating system when a process is launched to identify that particular process instance.

1. Enter the command **ps -u andy** to see all running processes for the user named "andy" – the latest process has a PID of **20749** and is running the **vi** text editor

2. Enter the command **ps -u dave -H** to see all running processes hierarchically for the user named "dave"– the latest process has a PID of **21116** and is running the interactive **ftp** file transfer facility

3. Assume root superuser status by entering the **su** command and the root password

4. Now issue the command **kill 21116** to terminate the **ftp** process – returning that user's terminal to a shell prompt

5. Enter an **exit** command to return to user status

Hot tip

To discover if a particular user is running one specific application, pipe the output from **ps -u** to **grep** – for example, **ps -u dave | grep ftp**.

```
Terminal                                    _ □ ✕
File  Edit  View  Terminal  Tabs  Help
user> ps -u andy
  PID TTY          TIME CMD
20664 pts/2    00:00:00 su
20665 pts/2    00:00:00 bash
20749 pts/2    00:00:00 vi
user> ps -u dave -H
  PID TTY          TIME CMD
21094 pts/0    00:00:00 su
21097 pts/0    00:00:00   bash
21116 pts/0    00:00:00     ftp
user> su
Password:
root> kill 21116
root> exit
exit
user> █
```

You can display a concise summary of the current shell process of each logged-in user with the **w** command and its **-s** option, or specify a user name after **-s** to see only their current processes.

The summary begins with a header displaying the current time, the length of time the system has been running, and the total number of users. It also provides details of system loading for 1 minute, 5 minutes, and 15 minutes – the average number of processes ready to run in that time period. The entire header can be suppressed by adding a **-h** option to the **w** command, or displayed without process information by the **uptime** command.

The process information shows the user name along with the console (tty) number or terminal (pts) number, the length of time idle, and what the process is being used for.

6 Enter the **w -s** command to see a full process summary – notice that the user named "dave" has a desktop console running in one process and the **ftp** file transfer facility running in a process within a shell terminal window

7 Now enter **w -sh andy** to display only the current processes of a user named "andy", suppressing the summary header information – that user has a desktop console running in one process and the **vi** text editor running in a process within a shell terminal window

8 Issue an **uptime** command to see the summary header

141

```
┌──────────────────────────────────────────────────────────┐
│ ▣                        Terminal            _ □ ⊠        │
├──────────────────────────────────────────────────────────┤
│ File  Edit  View  Terminal  Tabs  Help                   │
│ user> w -s                                            ▲  │
│  19:29:05 up  9:04,  6 users,  load average: 0.00, 0.02, 0.07│
│ USER     TTY      FROM              IDLE WHAT             │
│ mike     tty7     :0                1.00s x-session-manager│
│ andy     pts/0    :21.0            29:09m vi              │
│ mike     pts/1    :0.0              1.00s w -s            │
│ dave     pts/3    :20.0           28:11m ftp             │
│ dave     tty9     :20             28:11m x-session-manager│
│ andy     tty10    :21             29:09m x-session-manager│
│ user> w -sh andy                                         │
│ andy     pts/0    :21.0           29:18m vi              │
│ andy     tty10    :21             29:18m x-session-manager│
│ user> uptime                                            │
│  19:29:19 up  9:04,  6 users,  load average: 0.00, 0.01, 0.07│
│ user>                                                 ▼  │
└──────────────────────────────────────────────────────────┘
```

Working with accounts

User accounts are administered by the superuser who can issue a **useradd** command followed by a user name to create a new user. Existing user accounts can be modified by the superuser with the **usermod** command or deleted by the **userdel** command.

A user's login password can be changed by the **passwd** command, and personal information details changed by the **chfn** command. Each user may employ these to change their own details or root can specify a user name to change any user's details. The **finger** command will show the personal details of any specified user.

Beware

Never change any aspect of the root user account.

 1 Enter the **su** command and root password to assume root superuser status, then issue the command **useradd tony** to create a new user named "tony"

2 Enter the command **usermod -l toni tony** to rename the user named "tony" to "toni"

3 Now enter the command **passwd toni** and set a login password for this user

4 Issue the command **chfn toni** then enter personal details for this user

5 Enter an **exit** command to return to user status, then issue the command **finger toni** to see that user's details

Don't forget

The user's personal information details are typically more extensive than the brief details in this example – they are simplified here for brevity.

```
                                    Terminal                        _ □ ✕
 File  Edit  View  Terminal  Tabs  Help
root> useradd tony
root> usermod -l toni tony
root> passwd toni
Enter new UNIX password:
Retype new UNIX password:
passwd: password updated successfully
root> chfn toni
Changing the user information for toni
Enter the new value, or press ENTER for the default
        Full Name []: Toni Smith
        Work Phone []: 555-1234
root> exit
exit
user> finger toni
Login: toni                         Name: Toni Smith
Office Phone: 555-1234
user>
```

A group is a set of user accounts whose rights can be modified simultaneously. The root superuser might, for instance, grant a group permission to access a previously inaccessible file – all users who are members of that group are then allowed access.

Any user can discover which groups they belong to with the **groups** command and the root superuser can specify a user name as its argument to reveal the group membership of that user. Root can also employ the **groupadd** command to specify the name of a new group, or **groupmod -n** to change the name of an existing group, or **groupdel** to delete a specified group.

A user can be added to an existing group with the **-G** option of the **usermod** command, stating the group name and user name as its arguments.

6 At a root prompt, enter the command **groups toni** to discover that this user is only a member of a group named "tony" – added when the user account was created

7 Enter the command **groupmod -n toni tony** to change the group name so it matches the modified login name

8 Issue the command **groupadd board** to create a new group named "board"

9 Now enter the command **usermod -G board toni** to make that user a member of the new group

10 Enter **groups toni** to see all groups of which this user is now a member

Hot tip

Group information is typically stored in a file at **/etc/group** that lists all group names together with a comma-separated list of users belonging to each group.

```
Terminal                                    _ □ ✕
File  Edit  View  Terminal  Tabs  Help
root> groups toni
toni : tony
root> groupmod -n toni tony
root> groupadd board
root> usermod -G board toni
root> groups toni
toni : toni board
root>
```

Setting access permissions

The **ls -l** long listing command reveals the access permissions of each item in the current directory as a string of ten characters at the beginning of each line. The first is a **d** for a directory, or a dash for a file. This is followed by sequential Read, Write and Execute permissions for the owning User, Group, and Others. Characters **r, w,** and **x** appear for those permissions that are set, otherwise a dash is shown.

In the listing below, a script may be Read and Executed by everyone and the owner (this user) may also Write to it. The owner can both Read and Write a text note but others may only Read it. Three other text files may only be Read or Written to by their respective owners – so this user cannot access them.

Hot tip

See page 58 for more on access permissions.

```
Terminal                                        _ □ X

File  Edit  View  Terminal  Tabs  Help
user> whoami
linda
user> ls -lt
total 20
-rwxr-xr-x 1 linda linda 444 2007-08-10 11:35 lindas-script
-rw-r--r-- 1 linda linda  26 2007-08-10 11:33 lindas-note
-rw------- 1 mike  mike   21 2007-08-10 11:11 mikes-text
-rw------- 1 dave  dave   19 2007-08-10 10:56 daves-text
-rw------- 1 andy  andy   16 2007-08-10 10:46 andys-text
user> groups
linda board
user> cat lindas-note
here are linda's notes...
user> cat mikes-text daves-text andys-text
cat: mikes-text: Permission denied
cat: daves-text: Permission denied
cat: andys-text: Permission denied
user>
```

Don't forget

Notice that this user is a member of the group named "board" that was created on the previous page.

Each set of permissions can also be described numerically where Read = 4, Write = 2 and Execute = 1. For instance, a value of 7 describes full permissions to Read, Write and Execute (4 + 2 + 1), 6 describes permissions to Read, Write (4 + 2), and so on.

Permissions can be changed at a shell prompt with the **chmod** command, stating the permission values and the file name as its arguments. For example, the command **chmod 777 myfile** sets full permissions for a file named "myfile" in the current directory. If you need to change permissions where you are not the owner you must first assume root superuser status with the **su** command.

The **chgrp** command can be used to change the group membership of a file by stating a group name and the file name as its arguments. Similarly, the **chown** command can specify a user name and the file name to change the user ownership.

1. Enter the **su** command and root password to assume root superuser status in order to change access permissions of files owned by other users

2. Issue the command **chmod 644 mikes-text** to additionally allow everyone to read this file

3. Enter **chmod 640 daves-text** to allow the group to read this file

4. Now enter **chgrp board daves-text** to change the group to one of which this user is a member – so this user may now read this file

5. Enter **chown linda andys-text** to change ownership of this file – so this user may now read it, then **exit** to user status

6. Issue an **ls -l** command to see the changes then read the files where access was previously denied

Beware

Do not fall into the habit of setting everything to permissions of 777 – use access permissions thoughtfully to maintain useful restrictions.

145

```
                            Terminal                    _ □ X
File  Edit  View  Terminal  Tabs  Help
user> su
Password:
root> chmod 644 mikes-text
root> chmod 640 daves-text
root> chgrp board daves-text
root> chown linda andys-text
root> exit
exit
user> ls -lt
total 20
-rwxr-xr-x 1 linda linda 444 2007-08-10 11:35 lindas-script
-rw-r--r-- 1 linda linda  26 2007-08-10 11:33 lindas-note
-rw-r--r-- 1 mike  mike   21 2007-08-10 11:11 mikes-text
-rw-r----- 1 dave  board  19 2007-08-10 10:56 daves-text
-rw------- 1 linda andy   16 2007-08-10 10:46 andys-text
user> cat mikes-text daves-text andys-text
Mike says "Welcome!"
Dave says "Howdy!"
Andy says "Hi!"
user>
```

Installing packages

The Advanced Packaging Tool (APT) is a command-line tool that automates the process of retrieving, configuring, and installing software packages. It relies upon repositories to locate software and resolve dependencies – so that the installation package will include any libraries required by the application.

The APT's **apt-get** command has several options with which to manage packages. It's useful to initially execute an **apt-get update** command, in order to update the list of available repository packages, before issuing an **apt-get install** command.

Once installed, a package can be upgraded to the latest version with an **apt-get upgrade** command, or removed by issuing an **apt-get remove** command.

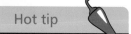

Hot tip

The Synaptic Package Manager is a user-friendly graphical interface for the Advanced Packaging Tool (APT) – see page 94 for more details.

 Enter the **su** command and root password to assume superuser status in order to install packages

 Issue an **apt-get update** command to ensure the package list is up to date

Now issue an **apt-get install** command to install a package, say the Gnome FTP client (gftp)

```
                          Terminal                    _ □ x
File  Edit  View  Terminal  Tabs  Help
root> apt-get install gftp
Reading package lists... Done
Building dependency tree
Reading state information... Done
The following extra packages will be installed:
  gftp-common gftp-gtk gftp-text
The following NEW packages will be installed:
  gftp gftp-common gftp-gtk gftp-text
0 upgraded, 4 newly installed, 0 to remove and 0 not upgraded.
Need to get 0B/525kB of archives.
After unpacking 3789kB of additional disk space will be used.
Do you want to continue [Y/n]? █
```

Beware

The **apt-get remove** command retains the configuration files. Use **apt-get --purge remove** for a complete removal.

 Note the names and size of the packages to be installed then type **Y** and hit Return if you are happy to proceed

146

```
□                       Terminal                    _ □ ✕
File  Edit  View  Terminal  Tabs  Help
Do you want to continue [Y/n]? Y                        ▲
Selecting previously deselected package gftp-common.
(Reading database ... 89454 files and directories currently install
Unpacking gftp-common (from .../gftp-common_2.0.18-16ubuntu3_i386.d
Selecting previously deselected package gftp-gtk.
Unpacking gftp-gtk (from .../gftp-gtk_2.0.18-16ubuntu3_i386.deb) ..
Selecting previously deselected package gftp-text.
Unpacking gftp-text (from .../gftp-text_2.0.18-16ubuntu3_i386.deb)
Selecting previously deselected package gftp.
Unpacking gftp (from .../gftp_2.0.18-16ubuntu3_all.deb) ...
Setting up gftp-common (2.0.18-16ubuntu3) ...
Setting up gftp-gtk (2.0.18-16ubuntu3) ...
Setting up gftp-text (2.0.18-16ubuntu3) ...
Setting up gftp (2.0.18-16ubuntu3) ...
root> █                                                ▼
```

Hot tip

The **apt-cache search** command is useful to locate package names.

After the packages are retrieved, unpacked, and set up, the installation is complete and the application is ready to run.

5 Type **exit** then hit Return, to return to regular user status, then issue the command **gftp** to launch the application

```
▤                       gFTP 2.0.18                    _ □ ✕
FTP  Local  Remote  Bookmarks  Transfers  Logging  Tools  Help
  🔷  Host: |        ▼  Port:  ▼  User:    ▼  Pass:    FTP  ↕  ⊗

/home/mike                    ▼      Not connected*              ▼
[Local] [All Files]                  ⬜ Filename      Size  User
⬆ Filename          Size  User  ➡
↩ ..              4,096  root
📁 .cache          4,096  mike
📁 .config         4,096  mike
📁 .evolution      4,096  mike
📁 .fontconfig     4,096  mike  ⬅
📁 .gconf          4,096  mike
📁 .gconfd         4,096  mike
📁 .gftp           4,096  mike
◀               ▶                    ◀                        ▶
Filename      Progress

```

Don't forget

You can use **man apt-get** to see the full range of options.

6 Close the application then launch it again using the item that has been added to the Applications, Internet menu

```
📗 Accessories      ▶
🎮 Games            ▶
🎨 Graphics         ▶
🌐 Internet         ▶    🔵 Ekiga Softphone
💻 Office           ▶    ✉ Evolution Mail
🔊 Sound & Video    ▶    🦊 Firefox Web Browser
                        🔲 gFTP
🔧 Add/Remove...         💬 Pidgin Internet Messenger
⚙ Applications  Places  🖥 Terminal Server Client
```

Getting the date and time

The **date** command displays the date, time, and timezone of the current locale. Optionally, the output from the **date** command can be formatted in several ways by adding format specifiers as its argument, such as the common date format specifiers in this table:

You can enter **man date** to discover the full range of date format specifiers.

Format specifier		Format specifier	
%A	Full day name	%a	Short day name
%B	Full month name	%b	Short month name
%D	Date as MM/DD/YY	%F	Date as YY-MM-DD
%H	Hours (0-23)	%I	Hours (1-12)
%M	Minutes (0-59)	%S	Seconds (0-60)
%R	Time as HH:MM	%T	Time as HH:MM:SS
%Y	Year	%Z	Timezone

1 At a shell prompt, enter the **date** command to see the date, time, and timezone at your locale

2 Enter **date +%A** to see today's full day name

3 Now enter **date +%D** to see the date numerically

4 Enter **date +%T** to see the current time

Hot tip

Format specifiers can be combined. For instance, date +%H:%M produces the same as date +%R.

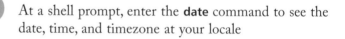

```
                        Terminal
 File  Edit  View  Terminal  Tabs  Help
user> date
Fri Aug 10 09:42:54 EDT 2009
user> date +%A
Friday
user> date +%D
08/10/09
user> date +%T
09:43:20
user>
```

148

The **cal** command usefully displays a calendar of the current month and highlights the current day. It can also take a year argument to display a calendar for that entire year.

 5   Enter a **cal** command to see this month's calendar

6   Now enter **cal 2010** to see a calendar for that entire year

```
user> cal
      August 2009
Mo Tu We Th Fr Sa Su
                1  2
 3  4  5  6  7  8  9
10 11 12 13 14 15 16
17 18 19 20 21 22 23
24 25 26 27 28 29 30
31
user> cal 2010
                        2010

      January                February                March
Mo Tu We Th Fr Sa Su   Mo Tu We Th Fr Sa Su   Mo Tu We Th Fr Sa Su
             1  2  3     1  2  3  4  5  6  7     1  2  3  4  5  6  7
 4  5  6  7  8  9 10     8  9 10 11 12 13 14     8  9 10 11 12 13 14
11 12 13 14 15 16 17    15 16 17 18 19 20 21    15 16 17 18 19 20 21
18 19 20 21 22 23 24    22 23 24 25 26 27 28    22 23 24 25 26 27 28
25 26 27 28 29 30 31                            29 30 31

       April                   May                    June
Mo Tu We Th Fr Sa Su   Mo Tu We Th Fr Sa Su   Mo Tu We Th Fr Sa Su
          1  2  3  4                 1  2        1  2  3  4  5  6
 5  6  7  8  9 10 11     3  4  5  6  7  8  9     7  8  9 10 11 12 13
12 13 14 15 16 17 18    10 11 12 13 14 15 16    14 15 16 17 18 19 20
19 20 21 22 23 24 25    17 18 19 20 21 22 23    21 22 23 24 25 26 27
26 27 28 29 30          24 25 26 27 28 29 30    28 29 30
                        31
        July                  August               September
Mo Tu We Th Fr Sa Su   Mo Tu We Th Fr Sa Su   Mo Tu We Th Fr Sa Su
          1  2  3  4                       1           1  2  3  4  5
 5  6  7  8  9 10 11     2  3  4  5  6  7  8     6  7  8  9 10 11 12
12 13 14 15 16 17 18     9 10 11 12 13 14 15    13 14 15 16 17 18 19
19 20 21 22 23 24 25    16 17 18 19 20 21 22    20 21 22 23 24 25 26
26 27 28 29 30 31       23 24 25 26 27 28 29    27 28 29 30
                        30 31
      October               November               December
Mo Tu We Th Fr Sa Su   Mo Tu We Th Fr Sa Su   Mo Tu We Th Fr Sa Su
             1  2  3     1  2  3  4  5  6  7           1  2  3  4  5
 4  5  6  7  8  9 10     8  9 10 11 12 13 14     6  7  8  9 10 11 12
11 12 13 14 15 16 17    15 16 17 18 19 20 21    13 14 15 16 17 18 19
18 19 20 21 22 23 24    22 23 24 25 26 27 28    20 21 22 23 24 25 26
25 26 27 28 29 30 31    29 30                   27 28 29 30 31
user>
```

Hot tip

You can also use the command **cal -3** to see a three-month calendar – showing the current month, previous month, and next month.

Summary

- Files can be compressed with **gzip**, **bzip2**, or **zip**, and uncompressed with their companions **gunzip**, **bunzip2**, or **unzip**

- Backup archives can be created using the streaming **cpio** command or the popular **tar** command

- The **df** command displays the free space of filesystems mounted on the Linux tree

- Filesystems may be manually attached to the tree with the **mount** command and detached with the **umount** command

- The **fsck** command checks a specified filesystem for integrity

- Each process has a unique Process ID (PID), revealed by the **ps** command, and may be terminated by a **kill** command

- The **w** command displays a concise summary of current shell processes and the **uptime** command can display its header

- User accounts can be created and edited by the root superuser with the commands **useradd**, **userdel** and **usermod**

- Login passwords can be changed with the **passwd** command and personal **finger** details edited with the **chfn** command

- The **groups** accounts can be created and edited by the root user with the commands **groupadd**, **groupdel** and **groupmod**

- Access permissions can be modified using the **chmod** command, and ownership changed using **chown** and **chgrp**

- The Advanced Packaging Tool (APT) list of available packages can be updated with the command **apt-get update**

- Packages can be installed from the command-line with the command **apt-get install** and removed with **apt-get remove**

- The **date** command has many format specifiers to output date components and the **cal** command displays useful calendars

9 Networking with the shell

This chapter demonstrates how to perform network tasks from the Linux shell and introduces scripting.

Connecting across a network

In much the same way that each house on a street has a unique address, to which mail can be addressed for direct communication, every computer on a network has a unique number, known as it's IP (Internet Protocol) address, which can be used to directly communicate with a particular computer.

You can discover the IP address of the computer behind a web address by stating the URL as the argument to the **host** command. In some cases, for large scale websites, this may reveal multiple IP addresses.

1 At a shell prompt, enter **host www.google.com** to discover the IP address for that URL

Hot tip

Add a **-a** option to a **host** command to see all information about that host.

```
Terminal
File  Edit  View  Terminal  Tabs  Help
user> host www.google.com
www.google.com is an alias for www.l.google.com.
www.l.google.com has address 64.233.183.104
www.l.google.com has address 64.233.183.147
www.l.google.com has address 64.233.183.103
www.l.google.com has address 64.233.183.99
user>
```

In Linux you can discover the IP address of your own computer by issuing the **ifconfig** command to display the network interface configuration. If your computer has multiple network connections each one will be listed separately.

You can supply the connection device name as the argument to the **ifconfig** command to see an individual report. Typically, if your computer connects to the network via an ethernet card the device will be called "eth0". If you are connected to a wireless network it will be called "ra0".

Beware

The **ifconfig** command only displays the status of active interfaces – add a **-a** option to include inactive interfaces.

2 If your network connection is via a cable plugged into your computer issue an **ifconfig eth0** command. If your network connection is wireless issue an **ifconfig ra0** command. Otherwise issue a plain **ifconfig** command to discover the network IP address of your computer.

```
┌─────────────────────────────────────────────────────┐
│ ▪                    Terminal              _ □ ✕     │
├─────────────────────────────────────────────────────┤
│ File  Edit  View  Terminal  Tabs  Help              │
│ user> ifconfig                                       ▲│
│ eth0     Link encap:Ethernet  HWaddr 00:48:54:1C:5D:95│
│          inet addr:192.168.0.101  Bcast:192.168.0.255 │
│          Mask:255.255.255.0                          │
│          inet6 addr: fe80::248:54ff:fe1c:5d95/65 Scope:Link│
│          UP BROADCAST RUNNING MULTICAST  MTU:1500  Metric:1│
│          RX packets:5891 errors:0 dropped:0 overruns:0 frame:0│
│          TX packets:3045 errors:0 dropped:0 overruns:0 carrier:0│
│          collisions:0 txqueuelen:1000                │
│          RX bytes:8125529 (7.7 MB)  TX bytes:225276 (219.9 KB)│
│          Interrupt:11 Base address:0x4000            │
│                                                      │
│ lo       Link encap:Local Loopback                   │
│          inet addr:127.0.0.1  Mask:255.0.0.0         │
│          inet6 addr: ::1/128 Scope:Host              │
│          UP LOOPBACK RUNNING  MTU:16436  Metric:1    │
│          RX packets:132 errors:0 dropped:0 overruns:0 frame:0│
│          TX packets:132 errors:0 dropped:0 overruns:0 carrier:0│
│          collisions:0 txqueuelen:0                   │
│          RX bytes:6600 (6.4 KB)  TX bytes:6600 (6.4 KB)│
│                                                      ▼│
│ user>                                                │
└─────────────────────────────────────────────────────┘
```

Hot tip

The loopback interface is useful for testing network applications locally before live deployment.

The computer in this example has a network connection via an ethernet interface with an IP address of 192.168.0.101.

The most basic test to see if another computer is reachable across the network sends tiny data packets to its IP address using the **ping** command. This continues sending test packets until you stop it but you may limit the number of packets by adding a **-c** option stating the total number of packets to send.

 3 Enter the command **ping -c 3 64.233.183.104** to send three packets to this IP address – to see if it is reachable

Don't forget

The IP address used here is one of those for the Google URL – revealed by the **host** command in step one.

```
┌─────────────────────────────────────────────────────┐
│ ▪                    Terminal              _ □ ✕     │
├─────────────────────────────────────────────────────┤
│ File  Edit  View  Terminal  Tabs  Help              │
│ user> ping -c 3 64.233.183.104                       ▲│
│ PING 64.233.183.104 (64.233.183.104) 56(84) bytes of data.│
│ 64 bytes from 64.233.183.104: icmp_seq=1 ttl=241 time=42.0 ms│
│ 64 bytes from 64.233.183.104: icmp_seq=2 ttl=241 time=39.6 ms│
│ 64 bytes from 64.233.183.104: icmp_seq=3 ttl=241 time=30.5 ms│
│                                                      │
│ --- 64.233.183.104 ping statistics ---              │
│ 3 packets transmitted, 3 received, 0% packet loss, time 2000ms│
│ rtt min/avg/max/mdev = 30.566/37.439/42.060/4.960 ms │
│ user>                                                │
│                                                      ▼│
└─────────────────────────────────────────────────────┘
```

Communicating on the network

The **telnet** program allows you to log into a remote computer where you have an account. Some community spirited computer systems allow anonymous **telnet** access – like that of the Seattle Community Network.

 Enter the **telnet** command to open the interactive telnet interface

 Now enter **open scn.org** to connect to the Seattle Community Network, then login as a visitor

```
Terminal                                            _ □ ✕
File  Edit  View  Terminal  Tabs  Help
user> telnet
telnet> open scn.org
Trying 66.212.64.194...
Connected to scn.org.
Escape character is '^]'.

Seattle Community Network Sun Solaris 1.1.1.B
Please login as 'visitor' if you are a visitor

SunOS UNIX (scn)

login: visitor
```

Hot tip

Hit return after logging in until you reach the main menu – then use the numbered menu choices to explore.

```
Terminal                                            _ □ ✕
File  Edit  View  Terminal  Tabs  Help
                <<< SEATTLE COMMUNITY NETWORK >>>
                     Main Menu (press M)

 1 Visitor and Information...    (registration, FAQ, donating)

 2 Help Menu...                  (confused? look here)

 3 Seattle Public Library...     (our good friends)

 4 E-mail Menu...                (read and send mail)

 5 World Wide Web...             (and local community web pages)

 6 Work with Your Files...       (file transfer, download)

 7 Settings and Utilities...     (terminal types, user lookup)

 8 Information Provider, Test, and Staff Menus
----------------------------------------------------------------
m = Main Menu        pine = Pine E-mail        h = Help
p = Previous Menu    lynx = Lynx Web Browser   x = Exit SCN

Your Choice ==> █
```

Typically with telnet the remote computer will be using a Unix-based operating system, like Linux, so will recognize bash shell commands for navigation – **cd, ls, pwd**, and so on.

Logging out from the remote computer can involve some guesswork as it depends which logoff command it uses – if unsure try "quit", "end", "exit", "close", "stop", "logout", and "logoff".

Telnet is quite an old program and unfortunately the data transmitted by telnet is only sent in plain text format – so it is easy for others to steal passwords and information. A more secure alternative is provided by the **ssh** secure shell command.

The **ssh** command encrypts all data that travels across the network including your user name and the password you will need to connect to the remote computer. It can also make sophisticated secure logins using public keys for user authentication. Once logged-in, **ssh** lets you execute commands on the remote machine.

3 To login to a remote machine named "example.com" where you have an account, enter the command **ssh example.com** – the first time you login you are asked to confirm that you wish to add that server to your list of known hosts by typing "yes"

4 Now enter your password for the remote machine and you will be placed at a shell prompt for that machine – where you can issue commands as normal

```
                    Terminal
File  Edit  View  Terminal  Tabs  Help
user> ssh example.com

mike@example.com's password: ********
Last login: Sun Aug 16 14:10:00 2009
Your operating system is Linux
Welcome to... the example domain
Checking your file quota... OK
mike@example.com->
```

Don't forget

The **ssh** command logs into the remote machine as the user name logged in on the local machine. To specify a different user name enter **ssh -l *username@domain***

155

Transferring files

You can send files over a network using File Transfer Protocol. The **ftp** command launches the interactive Ftp console where you can issue an **open** command to specify a hostname, or an IP address, to connect to your system. If the connected host is running a Unix-based operating system it will recognize bash shell commands for navigation – **cd**, **ls**, **pwd**, and so on.

The Ftp console recognizes **put** and **mput** commands to transfer single or multiple files from your computer to the connected host. Similarly, **get** and **mget** commands can be used to transfer single or multiple files from the connected host to your computer. Finally, you can use the **exit** command to close the Ftp console.

 At a shell prompt, enter the **ftp** command to start the interactive Ftp console

 At an Ftp console prompt, issue an **open** command specifying a host domain name to be connected

3 When asked, enter your user name and password to login to the connected host system

Hot tip

When logged-in to a remote system type **help** or **?** to see a list of commands it will accept.

```
                        Terminal                         _ □ X
 File  Edit  View  Terminal  Tabs  Help
user> ftp upload.ntlworld.com
Connected to upload.ntlworld.com.
220-
220-############################################################
220-
220-                Welcome to upload.ntlworld.com
220-
220-############################################################
220-
220 upload.ntlworld.com FTP server ready
Name (upload.ntlworld.com:mike): mike
331 Password required for mike.
Password:
230 User mike logged in.
Remote system type is UNIX.
Using binary mode to transfer files.
ftp> █
```

4 Enter **mkdir temp** to create a new directory named "temp" on the remote computer, then **cd temp** to navigate there

5 To transfer a file named "books.txt" from the current local directory to the new remote directory enter **put books.txt**

```
Terminal                                    _ □ ✕
File  Edit  View  Terminal  Tabs  Help
ftp> mkdir temp
257 "/temp" - Directory successfully created
ftp> cd temp
250 CWD command successful.
ftp> put books.txt
local: books.txt remote: books.txt
200 PORT command successful.
150 Opening BINARY mode data connection for books.txt.
226 Transfer complete.
210 bytes sent in 0.00 secs (1206.3 kB/s)
ftp> ▮
```

Don't forget

The **mget** and **mput** commands take a space separated list of files as their arguments.

6 Enter **rename books.txt morebooks.txt** to rename the file

7 Now enter **get morebooks.txt** to transfer the renamed file from the connected system to the local computer

8 Issue a **quit** command to close the Ftp console

9 Enter **cat morebooks.txt** to display the contents of the transferred file on standard output

```
Terminal                                    _ □ ✕
File  Edit  View  Terminal  Tabs  Help
ftp> rename books.txt morebooks.txt
350 File or directory exists, ready for destination name.
250 rename successful.
ftp> get morebooks.txt
local: morebooks.txt remote: morebooks.txt
200 PORT command successful.
150 Opening BINARY mode data connection for morebooks.txt (210 byte
226 Transfer complete.
210 bytes received in 0.02 secs (9.3 kB/s)
ftp> quit
221 Goodbye.
user> cat morebooks.txt
C Programming in easy steps
C++ Programming in easy steps
CSS in easy steps
HTML in easy steps
Java in easy steps
JavaScript in easy steps
PHP & MySQL in easy steps
Visual Basic in easy steps
XML in easy steps
user>
```

Beware

The get command will overwrite a file of the same name in the current local directory without warning!

Switching shell consoles

Unix, from which Linux is derived, was introduced long before graphical interfaces became popular. It was a text-based platform that used only a keyboard for input and displayed output on a simple monitor. The term "console" describes the combination of one input device (keyboard) and one output device (monitor).

Linux supports the notion of "virtual consoles" that let you have several full-screen shell sessions active simultaneously. You can easily switch between these using special key combinations. This is useful when you're working with multiple shell programs.

Most Linux installations provide seven virtual consoles by default although you normally only see the seventh – this is the one on which the X Window System is running the graphical desktop. The virtual consoles numbered 1 through 6 do not support graphics. They are, instead, configured to let you execute commands and to run shell programs.

To open a specific virtual console from the graphical desktop hold down the **Ctrl+Alt** keys with one hand and press one of the keys **F1** through **F6** with your other hand – **F1** will open virtual console number one, **F2** will open virtual console number two, and so on. Enter your user name and password to login to the console. To return to the graphical desktop at any time press **Ctrl+Alt+F7**.

Use the **who** command to discover which of the six text-based virtual consoles are being used. In the screenshot below the user is logged into virtual consoles one (tty1), two (tty2) and three (tty3) – each could be running different shell programs, or different instances of the same program.

Don't forget

In this example tty7 is running the graphical desktop and the user has a shell terminal window open on pts/0.

```
                              Terminal
 File  Edit  View  Terminal  Tabs  Help
user> who
mike      tty1          2009-08-14 10:20
mike      tty2          2009-08-14 10:20
mike      tty3          2009-08-14 10:20
mike      tty7          2009-08-14 10:10 (:0)
mike      pts/0         2009-08-14 10:20 (:0.0)
user>
```

...cont'd

 1 Press **Ctrl+Alt+F1** to open virtual console number one, then login and enter **vi** to start the text editor

```
This is simple text that is being writen
using the vi text editor in a Linux shell.
~
~
~
~
```

 2 Press **Ctrl+Alt+F2** to open virtual console number two then login and enter **man vi** to see the vi man page

```
VIM(1)                                                    VIM(1)

NAME
       vim - Vi IMproved, a programmers text editor

SYNOPSIS
       vim [options] [file ..]
       vim [options] -
 Manual page vi(1) line 1
```

3 Press **Ctrl+Alt+F3** to open virtual console number three then login and enter **ftp** to start the Ftp program

```
220-
220-############################################################
220-
220-                 Welcome to upload.ntlworld.com
220-
220-############################################################
220-
220 upload.ntlworld.com FTP server ready
Name (upload.ntlworld.com:mike): █
```

4 Quit all three applications then enter an **exit** command at each prompt to logout of each console

5 Enter **Ctrl+Alt+F7** to return to the desktop, then enter **who** in the terminal to confirm the consoles are closed

```
Terminal
File  Edit  View  Terminal  Tabs  Help
user> who
mike     tty7        2009-08-14 10:10 (:0)
mike     pts/0       2009-08-14 10:20 (:0.0)
user>
```

Hot tip

To quit vi type **:q** and to quit man type **q**. To quit the Ftp program type **exit** at an ftp prompt – or simply press **Ctrl+C**.

159

Sending network messages

The **mesg** command controls whether messages can reach your shell terminal. Its **y** option will allow messages and its **n** option will deny messages. When used with neither option the **mesg** command will report whether messages are currently allowed.

A message can be sent to another logged-in user on the system by the **write** command – with the user name as its argument. When you issue a **write** command the shell switches into write mode so you can type your message. When it's complete you can simply press **Ctrl+D** to mark its end, sending it to the specified user.

 Press **Ctrl+Alt+F1** to open virtual console one, then login

 Issue a **mesg** command to discover if messages are allowed – if they are not enter **mesg y** to allow messages

```
user> whoami
mike
user> mesg
is n
user> mesg y
user> mesg
is y
```

 Press **Ctrl+Alt+F2** to open virtual console two, then login as a different user

 Issue a **mesg** command to discover if messages are allowed – if they are not enter **mesg y** to allow messages

```
user> whoami
linda
user> mesg
is n
user> mesg y
user> mesg
is y
```

 Enter a **write** command, specifying the name of the user logged-in at step one, opening write mode to compose a message to be sent to the specified user

Don't forget

This example simulates messaging in a multi-user environment to demonstrate the **mesg** and **write** commands.

Type the message, then press **Ctrl+D** to send it to the user

```
user> write mike
Hi Mike,
Please send over the working file. Thanks.
See you later...
user>
```

 Press **Ctrl+Alt+F1** to return to console one and see that the message has been received

```
user>
Message from linda@linux-desktop on tty2 at 12:42 ...
Hi Mike,
Please send over the working file. Thanks.
See you later...
EOF
```

Notice that the message header states which console the message was sent from. If the user is logged-in to more than one console the **write** command will, by default, send the message to the one with least idle time in the hope that the sender is still there. Alternatively, you may specify a particular console to send the message to as an argument to the write command.

 Issue a **who** command to discover the message sender is also logged-in on console three, then send a reply there

```
user> who
linda     tty1          2009-08-14 12:25
linda     tty2          2009-08-14 13:17
mike      tty3          2009-08-14 11:57
mike      tty7          2009-08-14 10:10 (:0)
mike      pts/0         2009-08-14 10:20 (:0.0)
user> write linda tty3
Hi Linda,
I have just put the working file in the common area.
Bye.
```

9 Press **Ctrl+Alt+F3** to open virtual console three, and see that the reply has been received on that console

```
user>
Message from mike@linux-desktop on tty1 at 13:21 ...
Hi Linda,
I have just put the working file in the common area.
Bye.
EOF
```

161

Printing from the shell

The **lpr** command takes a file name or path as its argument to establish a print job to send the specified file to the printer. Each job is placed in a queue awaiting transmission to the printer – when the job reaches the front of the queue data from the file is sent to the printer and gets printed.

You can examine jobs in the print queue with the **lpq** command – each job is automatically assigned a job number. A job can be removed from the queue, before it gets sent to the printer, using the **lprm** command together with its job number.

 At a shell prompt, enter **lpr hi-res.jpg** to create a print job – to print a large image file named "hi-res.jpg"

 Enter **lpr ballad.txt** to create another print job – to print the specified text file

 Issue an **lpq** command to see the current print queue

```
                              Terminal
 File  Edit  View  Terminal  Tabs  Help
 user> lpr hi-res.jpg
 user> lpr ballad.txt
 user> lpq
 PSC_1400_series is ready and printing
 Rank     Owner    Job      File(s)                Total Size
 active   mike     2        hi-res.jpg             2636800 bytes
 1st      mike     3        ballad.txt             45056 bytes
 user>
```

The print queue reveals that the printer is actively printing job number two – the large image file.

 Before print job number two completes issue the command **lprm 2** to remove that job from the queue.

The printer halts that job without completing the print and moves onto to start printing the next job in the queue – the text file in job number three.

Beware

A print job can only be removed from the print queue by its owner or the root superuser.

Printing from a shell prompt is not restricted to simply printing files – data can also be queued for printing using the **lpr** command together with the **|** pipe character.

5 Issue the command **ls -l /etc | lpr** to print a list of the contents of the **/etc** directory – by piping the results of an **ls** command to the **lpr** command

6 While the directory content list is printing, issue an **lpq** command to see the print queue – stating the print source as piped from standard input

```
                            Terminal                    _ □ ✕
File  Edit  View  Terminal  Tabs  Help
user> ls -l /etc | lpr
user> lpq
PSC_1400_series is ready and printing
Rank   Owner   Job    File(s)              Total Size
active mike    4      (stdin)              13312 bytes
user>
```

The ability to print in Linux is provided by the Common Unix Printing System (CUPS). This provides a print spooler, which buffers data in a format the printer will understand, and a scheduler, which sends the buffered data to the printer when its ready to be received.

The **lpstat** command has individual options to provide CUPS status information about the scheduler, spooler, and printer/s.

7 Issue the command **lpstat -t** option shows all status information

```
                            Terminal                    _ □ ✕
File  Edit  View  Terminal  Tabs  Help
user> lpstat -t
scheduler is running
system default destination: PSC_1400_series
device for PSC_1400_series: hp:/usb/PSC_1400_series?serial=CN62ID20R104DZ
PSC_1400_series accepting requests since Fri 02 Nov 2007 09:28:02 AM EDT
printer PSC_1400_series now printing PSC_1400_series-5.
        both pens have low ink
PSC_1400_series-5       mike        2636800   Fri 02 Nov 2008 09:28:02
user> ▮
```

Hot tip

Where more than one printer is available use **lpr -P** to nominate the printer to print the job.

Don't forget

The status of the printer's ink cartridges can be seen with the **lpstat** command – here they are low on ink.

Evaluating expressions

The **expr** command enables you to perform simple math calculations at the shell prompt. It recognizes all the usual arithmetic operators but those which have other meanings in the shell need to be prefixed by a backslash \ escape character. For instance, the * wildcard must be escaped for multiplication.

Each argument must be separated by whitespace, and parentheses can be used to establish operator precedence in longer expressions – but each parenthesis character must be escaped.

The **expr** command can also perform boolean evaluations that return either true (1) or false (0) answers, and perform simple string manipulation with functions **length**, **substr**, and **index**.

 At a shell prompt, enter **expr 7 + 3** to perform addition and **expr 7 * 3** to perform multiplication

 Enter **expr 7 * \(3 + 1 \)** to evaluate a complex expression and **expr 7 = 3** to make a boolean equality evaluation

3 Issue the command **expr length "Linux in easy steps"** to discover the length of the specified string

4 Issue the command **expr substr "Linux in easy steps" 7 13** to extract a substring of the specified string

5 Issue the command **expr index "Linux in easy steps" "x"** to discover the position of the first "x" in the string

Don't forget

The arithmetic operators are + add, - subtract, * multiply, / divide, and % modulus.

Hot tip

You can quickly launch a calculator from a graphical terminal window using the **xcalc** command.

```
Terminal
File  Edit  View  Terminal  Tabs  Help
user> expr 7 + 3
10
user> expr 7 \* 3
21
user> expr 7 \* \( 3 + 1 \)
28
user> expr 7 = 3
0
user> expr length "Linux in easy steps"
19
user> expr substr "Linux in easy steps" 7 13
in easy steps
user> expr index "Linux in easy steps" "x"
5
```

The result of an expression evaluation can be made to cause a particular action using an **if-then-else** statement. This has three separate parts that specify a test expression, the action to perform when the test is true, and the action to perform when it is false.

The **if** keyword begins the statement and is followed by the test expression enclosed within a pair of **[ ]** square brackets. Each part of the entire statement must be separated from the next by whitespace to enable the shell to evaluate the expression.

The **then** keyword begins the second part of the statement, specifying the commands to execute when the test is true. Similarly, the **else** keyword begins the third part of the statement, specifying the commands to execute when the test is false. Finally, the **fi** keyword must be added to mark the end of the statement.

You may type the first part of the statement then hit Return to be prompted to enter the rest of the statement, or type the entire statement separating each part with a semicolon.

Beware

You must leave a space after the **if** keyword to avoid an error. Also leave a space after the **[** bracket and before the **]** bracket to avoid an error.

6 Type **if [`expr 7 % 2` = 0]** to test if the remainder of dividing seven by two is zero, then hit Return

7 At the statement prompt, enter **then echo "Even number"**

8 Now enter **else echo "Odd number"**

9 Type **fi** then hit return to perform the appropriate action

10 Make a similar test in a continuous statement by typing **if [`expr 8 % 2` = 0]; then echo even; else echo odd; fi** then hit return to perform the appropriate action

Don't forget

The backtick ` operators enclose **expr 7 % 2** so that operation gets performed before the test expression is evaluated – in this case the remainder of one is substituted making the expression **if [1 = 0]**.

```
                        Terminal                     _ □ ✕
File  Edit  View  Terminal  Tabs  Help
user> if [ `expr 7 % 2` = 0 ]
> then echo "Even number"
> else echo "Odd number"
> fi
Odd number
user> if [ `expr 8 % 2` = 0 ];then echo even;else echo odd;fi
even
user> █
```

Scripting for the shell

Lengthy shell routines, like those on the previous page, can be conveniently saved as a shell script for execution when required. Shell scripts are simply plain text files that begin their first line with **#!/bin/bash**, specifying the location of the bash program, and are typically given a **.sh** file extension.

Once a shell script file has its access permission set to "executable" it can be executed at any time by prefixing its name or path with the **./** dot-slash characters at a shell prompt.

A script might, perhaps, employ the **$RANDOM** shell variable that generates an integer from zero to 32,767 each time it is called. These are not truly random, however, as the same sequence is generated given the same starting point (seed) – in order to ensure different sequences it is necessary to set it with different seeds.

One solution is to extract a dynamic value from the current time using the **date +%s** command to deliver the current number of seconds that have elapsed since **00:00:00 GMT January 1, 1970**. Using this to seed the **$RANDOM** variable gets better random number generation.

Arithmetic can be performed on shell variables, such as **$RANDOM**, by including the **let** command in a script.

1. Open any plain text editor and begin a new file with the line **#!/bin/bash**

2. On a new line, type a line to seed the **$RANDOM** variable
   RANDOM=`date +%s`

3. Add a line to assign a value 1-20 to a variable
   let NUM=($RANDOM % 20 + 1)

4. On the next line type an instruction to clear the window
   clear

5. Add these lines to output text for the user
   echo "I have chosen a number between 1 and 20"
   echo "Can you guess what it is?"

Hot tip

Enter **RANDOM=1** then **echo $RANDOM** three times to see the pattern. Repeat the commands to see the pattern repeat.

Don't forget

You must not introduce whitespace around the = character in the assignments.

6 Now add a line to read the user's guess into a variable
read GUESS

7 Type the following lines exactly to evaluate whether the user's guess matches the generated number and output an appropriate response for each incorrect attempt

```
while [ $GUESS -ne $NUM ]
do
        if [ $GUESS -gt $NUM ]
                then echo "No - try lower... "
                else echo "No - try higher... "
        fi
        read GUESS
done
```

Hot tip

The **while-do** statement is a loop that employs the **-ne** (not equal) comparison operator and a **-gt** (greater than) comparison operator. Other bash shell comparison operators include **-eq** (equal) and **-lt** (less than).

8 Add a line to confirm a correct guess
echo "Yes the number is $NUM"

9 Save the script as **guess.sh** in the current directory

10 At a shell prompt change the access permissions to make the script executable by its owner with this command
chmod 711 guess.sh

11 Enter **./guess.sh** to execute the script

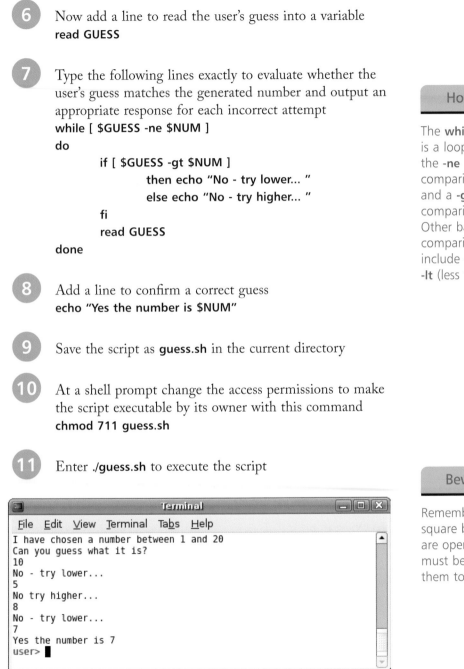

Beware

Remember that the square bracket characters are operators – there must be space around them to avoid errors.

Summary

- The IP address of a URL can be discovered with the **host** command and that of your own computer with **ifconfig**

- A network connection can be tested with the **ping** command

- The **telnet** program and **ssh** program let you login to a remote computer where you have an established account

- Files can be transferred over a network using the interactive Ftp program that is launched with the **ftp** command

- The **who** command displays a list of user names, consoles and terminals in current use

- Key combinations of **Ctrl+Alt+F1-7** switches between consoles

- The **mesg** command determines whether other users can send messages to you – and the **write** command can send a message from you to another user

- Print jobs are created with the **lpr** command and removed with the **lprm** command

- The current print queue can be displayed by the **lpq** command and CUPS status displayed by the **lpstat** command

- Expressions can be evaluated at a shell prompt by the **expr** command, which can also perform simple string manipulation using the **length**, **substr**, and **index** functions

- An **if-then-else** statement evaluates a test expression then performs an appropriate action

- Bash shell scripts are plain text files whose first line is **#!/bin/bash** and are typically given a .**sh** file extension

- A script can be executed at a shell prompt by prefixing its file name by .**/** the dot-slash characters

- The **$RANDOM** shell variable generates a sequence of pseudo-random numbers and can be seeded by **date +%s** to generate more random sequences

10 Command reference

This chapter provides an alphabetical listing of popular shell commands, options, and keywords.

Symbols

<	direct input from a file to a command
	eg: wc < some.txt
>	direct output from a command to a file
	eg: ls > ls.txt
>>	append output from a command to a file
	eg: date >> ls.txt
|	redirect (pipe) the standard output of one command to the standard input of another
	eg: echo sunny day | tr "a-z" "A-Z" – sends the output of the echo command to the tr command for translation to uppercase
;	combine commands
	eg: ls ; date
\	escape the following special character
	eg: echo Prompt\>
./	execute a script in the current directory
	./script.sh
..	parent directory
	eg: cd ..
~	alias for the home directory
	eg: cd ~
$	variable prefix to reference its stored value
	eg: echo $VAR
^C	(Ctrl+C) kill a running process
	eg: ping google.com ^C
^Z	(Ctrl+Z) suspend a running process
	eg: ftp ^Z
^D	(Ctrl+D) End Of Data marker
	eg: write *UserName* *Message* ^D

Hot tip

Multiple actions can be performed by joining several commands together with the | symbol – to create a "pipeline".

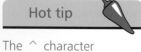

Don't forget

The commands and options listed in this chapter provide a handy reference for common operations, but this is not an exhaustive list – you can consult the man pages for further details on any command or use its --help option.

Hot tip

The ^ character represents the Ctrl key – so ^D represents pressing the Ctrl+D keys.

A - C commands

alias	create a command alias
	eg: alias HOME="cd ~"
apt-get	add or remove a package, update available list
	eg: apt-get install gftp eg: apt-get remove gftp eg: apt-get update
aspell	interactively check and correct spelling
	eg: aspell -c some.txt
awk	match data in a file to a regular expression
	eg: awk "{ print $2 }" some.txt - displays the second word of each line
basename	print the final part of a file path
	eg: basename /home/user/some.txt
bg	run a suspended job in the background
	eg: bg %2
bunzip2	uncompress a file from zip format
	eg: bunzip2 some.txt.bz2
bzip2	compress a file to zip format
	eg: bzip2 some.txt
cal	display a month calendar -3 option to display 3 months *Year* option to display 12 months
	eg: cal eg: cal 2010
cat	display the text content of one or more files
	eg: cat some.txt more.txt
cd	change working directory
	eg: cd /home/user eg: cd ~
chfn	change personal finger information
	eg: chfn -f *FingerName*
chsh (as root)	change the login shell program
	eg: chsh -s *UserName* /bin/ksh

Don't forget

Commands marked with "(as root)" should be run by the root superuser.

...continues overleaf

Beware

Changing ownership of files and directories will also change their accessibility.

Hot tip

You can set up crontab jobs to perform routine tasks that run each day, week, or month.

chgrp (as root)	change the group ownership of a file
	eg: chgrp *GroupName* /home/user/some.txt
chmod	change access permission of a file or directory for User, Group, and Others, where numerically Read = 4, Write = 2, and Execute = 1
	eg: chmod 640 some.txt
chown (as root)	change ownership of a file or directory
	eg: chown *UserName* /home/user/some.txt
	eg: chown :*GroupName* /home/user/Dir
cksum	print a CRC checksum number and byte count
	eg: cksum some.txt
clear	remove previous output from the shell display
	eg: clear
cmp	compare text or binary files, byte by byte
	eg: cmp some.txt more.txt
comm	compare text files, line by line
	eg: comm some.txt more.txt
cp	copy one or more files to another location
	eg: cp some.txt more.txt /tmp
crontab	run a recurring job at a specified time -l option to display the crontab file -e option to edit the crontab file -r option to remove the crontab file
	eg: crontab -l
csplit	split a file around specified expressions to produce separate files named xx00, xx01, etc.
	eg: csplit some.txt "/Part 1/" "/Part 2/" "Part 3/"
cut	get text from a file by column or delimited field -c option to specify a colum number -d option to specify a field delimiter -f option to specify a field number
	eg: cut -c 5-7 columns.txt eg: cut -d, -f 5 commafields.txt

D - F commands

date	display the date and time "+%D" argument to display date numerically "+%T" argument to display time as hh:mm:ss
	eg: date eg: date '+%T"
dc	open the command line desk calculator p operator to print the result c operator to clear the calculator stack q operator to quit the desk calculator

	eg: dc
	   6 4 * p
	   24

df	display file system free space -m option to list sizes in Mb, rather than Kb
	eg: df -m
diff	compare two text files, line by line
	eg: diff some.txt more.txt
diff3	compare three text files, line by line
	eg: diff3 some.txt more.txt next.txt
dir	display directory contents
	eg: dir
dircolors	list color settings for the ls command
	eg: dircolors
dirname	print the first part of a file path
	eg: dirname /home/user/some.txt
du	display disk usage of directories or files -h option to display human readable units
	eg: du -h some.txt eg: du -h /home/user
echo	display input on standard output
	eg: echo $SHELL
ed	open a file in a line-oriented editor
	eg: ed some.txt

Don't forget

The syntax required by the desk calculator is unusual. You can use the man dc command to open its man page and find more dc operators.

Hot tip

The ls colors database can be copied to a file in your home directory with dircolors -p > *file* for editing. Change a line in .bashrc so it reads dircolors -b *file* to use those colors in the shell.

...continues overleaf

...cont'd

Don't forget

The PS1 environment variable stores the command prompt format and colors.

Beware

In the expr example, the * character must be escaped for multiplication – otherwise it will be seen as a wildcard * operator.

egrep	match a specified string or regular expression using an extended version of grep
	eg: egrep *String* some.txt
eject	open the cd/dvd drive tray -t option closes an open tray
	eg: eject
env	display the environment variables
	eg: env
eval	construct a command from arguments
	eg: LSHOME="eval cd ~ ; ls -l"
exit	quit the shell or logout
	eg: exit
expand	convert tabs to spaces writing standard output
	eg: expand -t 3 tabs.txt
export	set an environment variable
	eg: export PS1=Prompt\>
expr	evaluate an expression
	eg: expr 7 * 3
factor	display prime factors of a specified number
	eg: factor 26
fdformat	low-level floppy disk format
	eg: fdformat /dev/fd0
fdisk (as root)	manipulate the hard disk drive partitions
	eg: fdisk /dev/hda
fg	run a suspended job in the foreground
	eg: fg %2
file	determine the file type
	eg: file some.txt
find	find a file in a specified hierarchy
	eg: find ~ -name "some*"

F - I commands

finger	display personal user information
	eg: finger *UserName*
fmt	format paragraph text on standard output -u option to provide uniform word spacing
	eg: fmt -u para.txt
fold	wrap standard output text at a specified width
	eg: fold -w 10 para.txt
for	perform a loop

	eg: for X in 1 2 3
	    do echo $X
	    done

free	display free disk space in Mb units
	eg: free -m
fsck (as root)	check and optionally repair file system
	eg: fsck
ftp	interactive file transfer via File Transfer Protocol

	eg: ftp *WebServerURL*
	    [Connected] Name: *UserName*
	    Password: *UserPassword*
	    put *FileName*
	    get *FileName*
	    quit

grep	match a specified string or regular expression
	eg: grep *String* some.txt
groups	display group names to which a user belongs
	eg: groups
groupadd (as root)	create a new group -f option to check group does not already exist
	eg: groupadd -f *GroupName*
groupdel (as root)	delete an existing group
	eg: groupdel *GroupName*
groupmod (as root)	change the name of an existing group
	eg: groupmod -n *NewName OldName*

Don't forget

The ~ alias can be used to find a file in your entire home directory – but remember to enclose the file name within quotes when issuing the find command.

Beware

Your user name and password is transmitted as plain text with ftp – the sftp command provides better security.

...continues overleaf

...cont'd

Hot tip

Compressed files that have the common .zip extension can also be uncompressed with gunzip.

Beware

There must be space around the square brackets in the if statement.

gunzip	uncompress a file from gzip format
	eg: gunzip some.txt.gz
gzip	compress a file to gzip format
	eg: gzip some.txt
hash	list commands memorized in this shell session
	eg: hash
head	output the first ten lines of a file -n option to specify a different number of lines
	eg: head -n 4 some.txt
history	display a list of commands in this shell session
	eg: history
hostname	display the name of the host computer
	eg: hostname
id	display user and group id numbers
	eg: id
if	perform a conditional test

	eg: if [$NUM -gt 5]
	    then echo "Greater"
	    else echo "Less"
	    fi

ifconfig	display the network interface configuration
	eg: ifconfig
init (as root)	change the system run level level 1 for maintenance console level 5 for normal GUI desktop
	eg: init 1
info	show help page for a command hit the Q key to return to a prompt
	eg: info ls
install	copy files, setting ownership and permissions -o option (as root) to specify ownership
	eg: install *SourceFiles* /usr eg: sudo install -o *SourceFiles UserName* /usr

J - L commands

jobs	display the status of all jobs
	eg: jobs
kill	terminate a job by number, or a process by PID
	eg: kill %2
	eg: kill 10436
last	display login history in chronological order
	eg: last
less	display content, page by page
	use Page Down and Page Up keys to move
	hit the Q key to return to a prompt
	eg: less long.txt
ln	create a hard link to a file
	-s option to create a symbolic soft link
	eg: ln ~/some.txt
	eg: ln -s ~/more.txt
login	log in and out of a low-level shell
logout	eg: login *UserName*
logname	display the user's login name
	eg: logname
look	display a list of words matching a given prefix
	eg: look *Prefix*
lpr	send a file to the printer
	eg: lpr some.txt
lprm	remove a print job from the printer queue
	eg: lprm 3
lpq	display the print queue and printer status
	eg: lpq
ls	list the contents of the current directory
	-a option to include hidden files
	-l option to include access permissions
	-t option to order the list by time stamps
	eg: ls
	eg: ls -alt

Hot tip

Long files can be viewed with both the more and less commands – but only less allows backward movement.

Don't forget

Typically you don't need to use login and logout commands in a Terminal window on a GUI desktop.

M - N commands

man	show help page for a command hit the Q key to return to a prompt
	eg: man ls
md5sum	produce an MD5 checksum number -c option to validate file against a checksum
	eg: md5sum some.txt > SUM eg: md5sum -c SUM
mesg	discover if your terminal write access is enabled n option to disable write access y option to enable write access
	eg: mesg eg: mesg n
mkdir	make a new directory
	eg: mkdir *DirectoryName*
more	display content, one screen at a time
	eg: more long.txt
mount	mount a file system -l option to list all mounted file systems
	eg: mount -l eg: mount /dev/cd
mt	control magnetic tape drive -f option to nominate a mounted device operations include: status, rewind, erase, offline, and eod (move to end of data)
	eg: mt -f /dev/tape eod
mv	move or rename a file or directory
	eg: mv some.txt /tmp eg: mv some.txt old.some.txt eg: mv Documents Docs
nice	run a program with specific priority level argument in the range -20 (high) to 20 (low)
	eg: nice --20 ftp
nl	number lines of text in standard output
	eg: nl some.txt

Don't forget

Options for the mesg command are not prefixed by a hyphen – they are simply y or n.

Beware

The nice range is between positive 20 and negative 20 – notice the two hyphens in the argument.

P commands

passwd	change a user password

	eg: passwd
	    Changing password for user
	    (current) UNIX password :

paste	merge text as columns on standard ouput
	eg: paste nums.txt names.txt
ping	test if a remote host can be reached by sending small data packets and await response -c option to specify the number of pings
	eg: ping google.com eg: ping -c 3 google.com
pr	prepare text content for printing the default format provides a header with date, file path, page number, and 66-line pagination -n option to number each line of text -h option to specify a header
	eg: pr some.txt eg: pr -n -h "My File" some.txt
printenv	display the environment variables
	eg: printenv
printf	print formatted string on standard output by substituting arguments of various data types %s to format a string argument %d to format an integer argument %f to format a floating-point argument %c to format a single character argument \n to include a newline character

	eg: printf "User %s is %d years old \n" Dave 13
	    User Dave is 13 years old
	eg: printf "Item %c cost $%0.2F \n" X 3
	    Item X cost $3.00

ps	display the process status
	eg: ps
pwd	print working directory
	eg: pwd /home/user

Hot tip

The ping command can accept URL or IP addresses – for instance use google.com or the IP address 64.233.167.99.

Hot tip

The printf command emulates the printf() function found in the C programming language.

R commands

rcp	remotely copy files between two machines
	eg: rcp some.txt host2:/home/user/some.txt – copies a local file to remote machine "host2"
read	read a line from standard input
	eg: read NAME Jack Frost echo "I read the name $NAME" I read the name Jack Frost
reboot (as root)	shutdown then restart the system
	eg: reboot
renice	change the priority level of a process PID that is already running with specific priority level argument in the range -20 (high) to 20 (low) – regular users can only decrease priority – the root superuser can also increase priority
	eg: renice 5 23402 23402: old priority 0, new priority 5
(as root)	eg: renice -3 23402 23402: old priority 5, new priority -3
rm	remove files or recursively delete directories -i option to ask before deleting each file -r option to a delete directory and its contents
	eg: rm some.txt eg: rm -ri *DirectoryName*
rmdir	remove an empty directory – use the rm command to delete non-empty directories
	eg: rmdir *DirectoryName*
rsync	remotely copy files betwen machines
	eg: rsync some.txt host2:/home/user/some.txt – copies a local file to remote machine "host2"

Don't forget

You can use the ps command to get the PID (process ID number) to specify the process to be changed by the renice command.

180

Beware

Always use the -i option with the rm -r command to recursively delete directory contents with individual confirmation requests – to avoid accidentally deleting required files.

S commands

scp	securely copy files between two machines – encrypting transmission and requesting passwords where required (unlike rcp)
	eg: scp some.txt host2:/home/user/some.txt – copies a local file to remote machine "host2"
sdiff	side-by-side comparison on standard output indicating line differences between two files

	eg: sdiff some.txt more.txt
	    chalk | cheese
	    match match
	    unique <
	          > unique

sed	match data in a file to a regular expression
	eg: sed "{ print $2 }" some.txt – displays the second word of each line
seq	print a sequence of numbers in a given range -w option to pad with leading zeros -s option to specify a separator
	eg: seq -w -s \\\| 4 12 04|05|06|07|08|09|10|11|12
sftp	secure file transfer via File Transfer Protocol
	eg: sftp *WebServerURL* [Connected] Name: *UserName* Password: *UserPassword* put *FileName* get *FileName* quit
shopt	display the shell behavior settings
	eg: shopt
shutdown (as root)	halts the system at a specified time or reboots -h option to halt now or after some minutes -c option to cancel a planned shutdown -r option to reboot
	eg: shutdown -h 0 eg: shutdown -h +5 eg: shutdown -r

Don't forget

In addition to sdiff comparison, files can be compared with the diff, diff3, and comm commands.

181

Hot tip

Root can issue the shutdown command with no options to immediately put the system at run level one – single-user maintenance mode.

...continues overleaf

sleep	pause for a specified number of seconds
	eg: sleep 3 – pauses for three seconds
sort	display lines of text sorted alphabetically
	eg: sort some.txt 　　Alpha 　　Bravo 　　Charlie – from original order Charlie, Bravo, Alpha
split	split a file into pieces of a specified size -l option to specify lines per output file
	eg: split -l 1 some.txt – creates files named xaa, xab, xac, etc. each containing one line copied from the source file
ssh	secure shell login to a remote machine where you already have an account -l option to specify your remote user name if different to your local user name
	eg: ssh -l *RemoteUserName RemoteServerURL*
stat	display the file statistics describing its byte size, access permissions, last modified, and more
	eg: stat some.txt
su	switch user to root or to a specified username
	eg: su eg: su *UserName*
sum	print a checksum number and block count
	eg: sum some.txt
suspend	suspend the current shell – returns to the user shell from a root shell
	eg: suspend
sync	flush all file system buffers to disk – only used to ensure nothing is held in memory before performing a risky operation
	eg: sync

Beware

The sum command only creates a short checksum number which may not be unique to that file! The cksum command produces a longer checksum, but the 32-byte checksum created by the md5sum command is far better.

Don't forget

A suspended root shell can be resumed using the fg command and its job number, taken from the jobs command list – for job number one use the command fg %1 to resume the root shell.

T commands

tac	view the text content of one or more files, in reversed line order
	eg: tac some.txt more.txt
tail	output the last ten lines of a file -n option to specify a different number of lines
	eg: tail -n 4 some.txt
tar	create, update, or extract from, a compressed tape archive file – also often gzipped -c option to create a new archive -z option to gzip or gunzip -u option to update an existing archive -x option to extract files from an archive -v option to see verbose descriptive output -f option to use the archive file
	eg: tar -czvf archive.tar.gz Folder/ eg: tar -uzvf archive.tar.gz some.txt eg: tar -xzvf archive.tar.gz
tee	print to both standard ouput and a file -a option to append, rather than overwrite
	eg: sort cba.txt | tee sorted.txt eg: sort zyx.txt | tee -a sorted.txt
test	evaluate a boolean expression and return the result as true (0) or false (1) in variable $? also optionally allows [ ] alias -d argument to test for directory -f argument to test for file = argument to test for string equality != argument to test for string inequality -eq argument to test for numeric equality -ne argument to test for numeric inequality -lt argument to test for lesser number -gt argument to test for greater number

	eg: test -d some.txt
	    echo $?
	    1
	eg: [5 -gt 3]
	    echo $?
	    0

Hot tip

The tar command can alternatively use bzip2 for zip compression – by using a -j option in place of the -z option.

183

Beware

When using the [ ] alias to make tests, each square bracket must be surrounded by space – adjacent characters would form a string and cause an error.

...continues overleaf

...cont'd

time	run a program and time its system resource use
	eg: time *ProgramName*
times	display the shell uptime and system uptime
	eg: times
touch	create a new empty file or update the timestamp of an existing file
	eg: touch *FileName*
top	list all processes running on the system -p option to monitor a specific PID
	eg: top eg: top -p *PIDnumber*
tr	translate one set of characters to another

	eg: echo sunny day | tr "a-z" "A-Z"
	    SUNNY DAY
	eg: echo happy frog | tr "frog" "toad"
	    happy toad

tty	print the name of the terminal device associated with the current shell
	eg: tty /dev/pts/0
type	determine a command type
	eg: type echo echo is a shell builtin
umask	prints or sets the user mask value that determines permissions of new files created – default mask value of 0022 allows the user read and write privileges and all others to read – mask 0002 allows the group read and write privileges and all others to read – mask 0077 allows the user read and write privileges and no privileges for all others
	eg: umask 0022
	eg: umask 0077

Beware

The tr command translates sets of characters – specify a replacement of the same number of characters.

Don't forget

New diectories created with the default umask 0022 allow the user full privileges and all others to read and execute.

U - V commands

umount	unmount a file system
	eg: umount /dev/cd
unalias	remove an alias
	eg: unalias *AliasName*
uname	display system information -a option to display all information -n option to display the host name -r option to display the kernel release
	eg: uname -a
unexpand	convert spaces to tabs writing standard output
	eg: unexpand spaces.txt
uptime	display system uptime
	eg: uptime
uniq	discard all but one identical lines of input
	eg: uniq repeat.txt
unzip	extract compressed files from a zip archive
	eg: unzip archive.zip
useradd (as root)	add a user account
	eg: useradd *UserName*
userdel (as root)	delete a user account
	eg: userdel *UserName*
usermod (as root)	modify a user account -p option to change the user password
	eg: usermod -p *NewPassword UserName*
users	list the name of users currently logged in
	eg: users
vdir	verbosely display directory contents
	eg: vdir
vi	launch the vi text editor – supply a file name to open at launch
	eg: vi eg: vi *FileName*

Beware

The command to unmount a file system is umount – no "n" after the "u".

Don't forget

With vi, hit Insert to enter Insert Mode and Esc to leave it. Type :w then hit Return to write the file and :q to quit.

W - Z commands

w	display current processes for each logged-in user
	eg: w
watch	execute a command at regular intervals -n option to specify number of seconds delay
	eg: watch -n 1 date "+%T"
wc	display word count, line count, and byte count
	eg: wc some.txt
wget	download a web page and store a local copy
	eg: wget http://www.ineasysteps.com
whereis	list source and man locations of a command
	eg: whereis ls
which	display the source file location of a program
	eg: which ftp
whoami	display the name of the current effective user
	eg: whoami
write	send a message to another logged-in user

	eg: write *UserName*
	    Message
	    ^D

xcalc	launch a graphical calculator from a shell window
	eg: xcalc
zcat	ouput compressed text on standard output
	eg: zcat some.txt.gz
zip	create a compressed archive in zip format
	eg: zip archive.zip *FileName FileName*

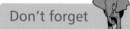

Don't forget

If a web download fails due to network problems wget will keep retrying until the whole file has been retrieved.

Hot tip

Unlike gzip and bzip2 the zip command does not delete the original files.

Index

R

S